SATAN'S SUPER SOLDIERS

OTHER BOOKS BY BARRY BLACKSTONE:

Though None Go With Me

Rendezvous In Paris

Though One Go With Me

Scotland Journey

The Region Beyond

Enlarge My Coast

From Dan to Beersheba and Beyond

The Uttermost Part

Homestead Homilies

Rover: A Boy's Best Friend

North to Alaska and Back

Another Day in Nazareth

Sermonettes from the Seashore

Earth's Farthest Bounds

Angling Admonitions

Beyond the Bend

Expendable

Meows from the Manse

At a Moment's Notice

Reaching the Unreached

SATAN'S SUPER SOLDIERS

The Giants of the Bible

by BARRY BLACKSTONE

RESOURCE *Publications* · Eugene, Oregon

SATAN'S SUPER SOLDIERS
The Giants of the Bible

Resource Publications
An Imprint of Wipf and Stock Publishers
199 W. 8th Ave., Suite 3
Eugene, OR 97401

www.wipfandstock.com

PAPERBACK ISBN: 979-8-3852-1229-3
HARDCOVER ISBN: 979-8-3852-1230-9
EBOOK ISBN: 979-8-3852-1231-6

VERSION NUMBER 041124

I DEDICATE THIS BOOK ABOUT **'GIANTS'** TO THE MAN AT EMMANUEL BAPTIST CHURCH IN ELLSWORTH, MAINE THAT GAVE ME THE IDEA TO FIRST WRITE THIS BOOK. A NUMBER OF YEARS AGO AFTER I SPOKE ON BIBLICAL GIANTS AT A MEN'S FELLOWSHIP BREAKFAST, CHARLES TROTTIER (Charlie was my car doctor for over 20 years) ENCOURAGED ME TO SHARE MORE INSIGHTS ON THIS THEME. HERE IS THE RESULT OF THAT RESEARCH ON SATAN'S SUPER SOLDIERS. THANKS TROTTIER FOR PROVOKING ME IN THIS STUDY; IT HAS HELPED ME A LOT IN MY OWN BATTLE WITH GIANTS IN MY LIFE!

CONTENTS

PRELUDE

SATAN'S SUPER SOLDIERS

Job 16:14-He breaketh me with breach upon breach, He runneth upon me like a GIANT.

I HAVE BEEN A serious student (II Timothy 2:15) of God's Word for 60 years now. Instead of studying the Bible from Genesis to Revelation (the Biblical order), I have been conducting my research by Barry's order. When one looks back on this order of study: there seems to be no rational rhyme or logical reason for the order. Only the Holy Spirit, which has been my teacher (I John 2:27), can explain fully why this has been the order I was directed into, a systematic study God's Scriptures: Titus, Philippians, Daniel, II Timothy, I Corinthians, I Thessalonians, Revelation, Jude, Genesis, Hosea, I John, John, Mark, Exodus, I Timothy, Leviticus, Joshua, Numbers, I Peter, II John, III John, Nehemiah, Song of Solomon, Judges, Hebrews, Philemon, Obadiah, Ruth, Esther, Colossians, Matthew, Acts, Proverbs, Haggai, Jonah, Habakkuk, Zephaniah, II Peter, James, II Thessalonians, Amos, II Corinthians, Psalms, Ecclesiastes, Romans, Galatians, Ephesians, Luke, Isaiah, Jeremiah, Lamentations, Ezekiel, Joel, Nahum, Ezra, Deuteronomy, Micah, Malachi, Zechariah, Job, I Samuel, II Samuel, I Kings, II Kings, I Chronicles, and II Chronicles. This was the order that I studied the 66 books of the Bible from 1973–2011. After that first study I restudied all 66 book again from 2011–2023, but this time I compiled a one-chapter summary on all 1189 chapters. Once that was done I have started again looking at each book and this time I am putting together a two-page outline of each chapter and a Powerpoint presentation on each of those chapters (I have 70 chapters done in 12 books at the last edit of this book). Only God knows if I will complete a third look at His Word, for despite these years of study, I am far from being an expert on any of the subjects recorded in the Word of God, but a few have been a fascination and I have spent a good deal of time digging a bit deeper into God's Word on certain topic; including the theme of this book (a twenty-five year exploration).

A case in point is the content of this book, *Satan's Super Soldiers*: the giants of the Bible. When I came to the verse I have printed at the head of this introduction, I decided I would search the Scriptures and find out what I could about these 'men of renown' (giants) (Genesis 6:4). I had been watching for the diabolical devices the Devil used against Job and realized that this was one of Satan's early strategies. **Job felt like a pygmy being run over by a giant**. It was then I realized in all my research into the Devil's devices (II Corinthians 2:11), I had missed 'giants'. I had studied the 'giants' before, but had not drawn the connection between Job and 'giants' until I was looking into Job's monumental temptation. I hear and read and watch as Christian after Christian seems to stand powerless against the onslaught of the Wicked One and his demons. However, through the Scriptures we have been forewarned of his attacks (Ephesians 6:10–12) and forearmed (Ephesians 6:13–18) to defeat every attack, including by giants. With a foreknowledge of their tactics we can forestall their advantages in strength and strategy and soldering. We don't have to be ignorant of their devices (II Corinthians 2:11) because God has spelled them out for us in His Holy Writ. This book is being written to define the satanic device the Bible calls 'giant', how to defeat them, how any one of us can be a 'giant killer'!

Interestingly, at the time of my decision to get this study published, the men's Bible study group at our church has been studying 'spiritual warfare' for over half a year now. I think it was that study that provoked me to dig out this old research and finally put it into book form. What I have discovered is that most today are ignorant of the spiritual fight that is raging all around us. Maybe we are not facing physically large men, but we are still facing the one that created these 'giants', and while the giants of today might seem smaller physically; they are still formable foes and we still have to face them.

Let me share this concept even before we start defining and describing the Biblical 'giants': **there is not recorded one occasion where a giant has ever defeated a man of God in battle.** Satan's super soldiers were never a match for God's warriors: no matters their size, strength, or how scary they could be. Satan came to understand this truth in time and stopped using 'giants' in the days of David, but by then he had used them for thousands of years. Also let us never forget, the greatest 'giant' of them all, Satan, is still on the loose seeking whom he may defeat and devour (I Peter 5:8), but like his 'giants' he too is defeatable (James 4:7). My prayer is a reading of these defeated 'giants' will help you to stand and withstand (Ephesians 6:13–14); even Satan's Super Soldiers!

1

GIANTS
A DEVICE OF THE DEVIL

II Corinthians 2:11-Lest **SATAN** should get an advantage of us: for we are not ignorant of his devices.

WE START OUR BOOK on 'giants' with a description of Satan's Super Soldiers by looking at the Devil's master strategy against God and His people. It is a three-pronged attack:

1. **First, Defeat the Lord.** Isaiah 14:13–14. This part of the Devil's program has not changes since the day he lifted up his heart to overthrow the throne of God (Revelation 12:7–9). He attacks God in three areas: A) He is trying to DEGRADE the PERSON of God-Genesis 3:1. B) He is trying to DISCREDIT the PLAN of God-Genesis 3:4. C) He is trying to DESTROY the PROCLANATIONS of God-Genesis 3:1. These tactics used in the Garden of Eden have not changed, and I challenge you to watch carefully when the Lord's people are under attack by someone, or something, if these are not the SAME tactics still being used today by the Devil and his demons and his demonic men: giant or no giant.

2. **Second, Damn the Lost.** II Corinthians 4:4. We know the Devil is going to the Lake of Fire eventually (Matthew 25:41), and he is determined to take as many with him as possible. How does he do that?

1

A) He DIVERTS their ATTENTION from the TRUTH-James 4:13, B) He DANGLES certain ATTRACTIONS of THINGS before them-I John 2:15–17, C) and He DELAYS their ACCEPTANCE of the TIME of salvation-Luke 12:13–20 and II Corinthians 6:2. Despite the fact that these tactics have been used on every generation since Adam and Eve, the Devil is still very successful with these well-known strategies. Who of us was not taken-in by one or more of these tactics before we found the Captain of our Salvation (Hebrews 2:10) in the person of Jesus Christ our Lord?

3. **Third, Disrupt the Christian.** II Corinthians 12:7 and I Thessalonians 2:18. It is in this arena that I am most concerned about today. Here is a list of some of the areas the Devil is using his devices to disturb and dismay and discourage the believer in Christ: A) the device of DROWSINESS-I Thessalonians 5:6, B) the device of DEATH-Hebrews 2:14–15, and C) the device of DEVOURING-I Peter 5:8, and the Devil can devour through STORMS-Job 1:19, through SICKNESS-Job 2:7, and through SUFFERING-Job 1:15, 16, 17.

We defeat these devices when we STAND UP (James 4:7) against him, and WAKE UP (I Peter 5:8) to the fact that we are under attack, and LOOK UP (Job 1:20) to the Lord for our strength and protection, and LIFT UP (James 1:2) our hearts in prayer, and finally GIVE UP, not to the Devil, but to the will of God and His Spirit that lives within us (I John 4:4). Once we see and understand his master plan, it helps us to know what part 'giants' played in his schemes against the people of God, especially in the Old Testament.

I have always been interested in 'giants' or 'nephilim' (Numbers 13:33), but it wasn't until I was studying the plight of Job that I realized that one of Satan's earliest diabolical devices was the use of 'giants' against God's people; though I believe that the race of 'giants' was finally wiped out by David and his mighty men: we still have much to learn about the strategy of Satan by taking a careful look into Satan's Super Soldiers. Who were they; what were they; where did they come from, and why were they so successful early on? This is what I have come to believe about the devilish device called "giant":

Genesis 6:4: "There were GIANTS in the earth in those days; and also after that, when the sons of God came in unto the daughters of men, and they bare children unto them, the same became **mighty men** which were of old, **men of renown.**"

1. **THE REALITY OF GIANTS.** The fact that 'giants', being of abnormal size, having lived on the earth is a very clear concept in Scripture. They lived in the days of Noah (in those days-Genesis 6:4) and the days of Job (also after that-Job 14:16) and the days of Abraham (Genesis 14:5–7) and the days of Moses (Deuteronomy 1:28) and of course the days of David (II Samuel 21:15–22). The most mentioned group of 'giants' were called Anakims (Deuteronomy 2:10–11, 21, 9:2). Another group of 'giants' were called Rephaims (Genesis 14:5). There is no doubt in Scripture that races of 'giants' did once exist.

2. **THE RACES OF GIANTS.** Genesis 6:4 is where all stories of Biblical 'giants begins. We have to start here to understand just who or what 'a giant' was? There seem to be two basic interpretations in Church teachings to explain the doctrine of 'giants'. The first view teaches us that the original race of 'giants' came about as a direct result of fallen angels (Jude 6 and II Peter 2:4) mating with the daughters of men producing a super race of half-humans and half-demons. The other view is that the natural production of man and woman over many generations eventually produced a master race of exceptional smart, strong, and superior size human beings: men of renown, mighty men, 'giants'? Whichever you believe, the debate is over at Noah's Flood! This super human race, or the demonic race was wiped out in the flood waters (perhaps, one of the reason for the need of the flood), but Moses, the author of Genesis, is very clear that somehow the giants survived, or were reintroduced after the flood: _**"...and also after that..."**_

3. **THE RESURGENTS OF THE GIANTS.** "And there we saw the GIANTS, the sons of Anak, which come of the GIANTS: and we were in our own sight as grasshoppers, and so we were in their sight." (Numbers 13:33) We know that only Noah and his family survived of the human race in the Flood (Genesis 7:23), yet we are confronted again with the 'giants' after the Flood. Interestingly, after the Flood, the only place that 'giants' are mentioned is in the context of the Promised Land. From Job to Abraham to Moses to David, the giants were found in the way of the Hebrew nation from fully claiming and conquering their Promised Land in Canaan. We see in this; the diabolical hand of the Devil. As you read through the Old Testament you will find the Devil trying to change the plan of God concerning the coming of His Son. Whether his tempting of Eve in Eden, or trying to wipe out the

Jews by the hand of Haman, Satan has been at the business of trying to change the outcome of God's Master plan of Redemption. If Satan could stop the Israelites from entering the land, he might keep the Saviour out of the world as well! Let us never forget that the primary reason the ten spies gave such a negative report after their exploration of Canaan was **"and we saw giants"**! For 40 years the fear and fright and fascination of 'giants' did kept the Israelites at bay, blocking them from entering the Land of Promise!

Despite the fact that there are no longer any physical 'giants' left in Satan's army; we are still confronted with giant issues and gigantic numbers and gargantuan emotions like doubt (remember, John Bunyan's giant) and fear that still keeps the people of God from advancing into promised places. God's people are still facing 'giants' to this day I believe, so it is vital that we know something about them and how to defeat them!

2

HOW WERE GIANTS CREATED?
PART ONE

Genesis 6:4-There were **GIANTS** in the earth in those days; and also after that, when the sons of God came in unto the daughters of men, and they bare children to them, the same became mighty men which were of old, men of renown.

In the Hebrew text there are three words that can be translated as 'giants' in our English Bible: GIBBOR-strong ones (Job 16:14), RAPHA-fearful ones (Deuteronomy 2:11), and NEPHILIM-fallen ones (Genesis 6:4). Most do not deny the claim of the Bible that there were 'giants' on the earth at one time or the other, but where the disagreement begins is at their beginning, creation if you will. Our text above is the only explanation given for the origin or appearance of 'giants in the earth'!

Two basic doctrines have emerged about 'giants' from the teaching of Jewish scholars and Church teachers. I find that there have been good people on both sides of this issue, and I have come to believe that the doctrine of 'giants' must fall under the classification of _**'doubtful disputations'**_ (Romans 14:1). Paul underlines the ground rule by which opposite view points are handled: **"Let every man be fully persuaded in his own mind."** (Romans 14:5) It is for this reason I share with you the two basic sides on the interpretation of 'giants', and leave with you the right to choose your own understanding and insight into the question, or maybe other concepts you might have on: so how were giants created; where did they start, and what is the source of these 'giants'?

First, what I like to call the conservative view about 'giants': when the 'sons of God', the godly descendants of Seth (Genesis 4:26) began to intermarry with the 'daughters of men', the ungodly descendants of Cain (Genesis 4:13) that a race of wicked men arose. Remember, the meaning for giants in Genesis 6:4 is 'fallen ones', or 'those who have fallen'-nephilim. Those on this side of the issue believe the word refers to the violent nature first seen in Cain (Genesis 4:8) and eventually becomes a characteristic of mankind (Genesis 6:13). In other words, the offspring of these who inter-married were mighty men of wickedness. Moses goes on to explain just how corrupt these 'giants' became: **"And God saw that the wickedness of man was great in the earth, and that every imagination of the thoughts of his heart was only evil continually."** (Genesis 6:5) The deepest form of wickedness described in any section of the Scriptures, and the ultimate depth that the depravity of man can go (Jeremiah 17:9)! Though I don't think we are there yet, the Lord said as the days of Noah so would the coming of the Son of Man be (Matthew 24:37), and we can certainly see in our day certain people have gotten so wicked that they are consumed by it whether in thought or action!

Not only were these men large in size as is suggested in the only other place this Hebrew word (nephilim) is found (Numbers 13:33-more later), but they were a terror (perhaps, the world's first terrorists) to all that came into contact with them. What God saw from these giants reveals a condemnation not mentioned again of anyone or any group in the rest of Scripture: total depravity, total corruption, and total wickedness. How corrupt? How depraved? How wicked? When the wicked become _'men of renown'_; when the most notorious sinner in the world becomes the most famous celerity in the world. When the bad are honored above the good; when the evil one is the respected one, things are pretty bad! God saw just how deep this wickedness went, to the very heart, to the core of man, and God knew there was no redemption possible and unless He did something the entire human race would be completely corrupted. I believe, not since God looked into the heart of Satan himself and his demons had He see such evil!

Jeremiah would write of this kind of heart this way: "The heart is deceitful above all things, and desperately wicked, who can know it?" (Jeremiah 17:9) Only God can know, and when He looked into the heart of these 'giants' He saw the bitter root of rebellion, the zenith of evil, the corrupting spring of wickedness, the violence and wantonness that would eventually control the whole world. On all three levels of the human mind: heart, thought, and imagination God only found *"evil continually"*. These 'giants' had gone beyond redemption; they were unredeemable, beyond salvation, without hope of regeneration. They like their father the devil (John 8:44) had fallen too far! No wonder the text would next proclaim: **"And it repented the Lord that he had made man on the earth, and it grieved Him at His heart."** (Genesis 6:6) Whether of Satan, directly or indirectly, his corrupting of mankind seemed to have worked and these 'giants' were the instrument Satan used in his diabolical plot to corrupt and condemn the human race before a Redeemer could come. They were not called soldiers here, just **'men of renown'**, 'mighty men' in business, invention, politics, etc., but Satan's soldiers don't always wear armor or uniforms, they can also be found in three-piece suits, athletic gear, or clergy robes! (II Corinthians 11:13–15)

By the 4th century of the Church this teaching became the primary instruction concerning 'giants' mainly to prevent the pagan worship of angels (Colossians 2:18-the other interpretation we will see in the next chapter). Men like Matthew Henry made this his teaching in his classic commentaries as did men like Scofield in his famous Bible. Their argument for this doctrine: the 'how' of giants has left me with four questions:

1. Why the union was only between the male descendants of Seth and the female descendants of Cain; why not the male and female of each involved as well?

2. Were all the descendants of Seth male and Cain female, and were all of Seth's descendant's believers and all of Cain's descendant's unbelievers?

3. How did the union of simple human beings result in a super race (remember Hitler tried this and it didn't work) of giants with unusual stature and amazing intelligence; not only titans physically, but mentally superior as well?

4. Why would simple intermarriage between spiritual opposites result in such corruption and wickedness and unbelievable evil and violence?

I will leave you with these questions and the suggestion that the first giants were a product of natural production and that in time they created through genetics a group of supermen (why not super women as well) and that in time (remember, **'men of old'**) they corrupted the whole world except for eight people (I Peter 3:20), and they were not pure (Genesis 9:20–24) by any means! Old age was defined in the hundreds of years (Genesis 5) back then, so there was time not only to grow corrupt, but to grow large if the climate and the makeup of man were different in the days before the flood. We do believe the age before the flood was much different than after, so with time these 'mighty men' could have emerged to command and control that first civilization. We have seen such men rise in our post-flood world; men, even great in stature, men great in power and influence who used violence to control their people, their lands, and for some the hope of dominating the world? For me, the lesson is clear. We too are on the doorstep of a time when another 'giant' among men (**The Antichrist**) will rise to become a mighty man in the earth; a man of renown who the world will not only follow but eventually worship. Who will for his time corrupt the whole world to such an extent that the prophecy of Jesus will be fulfilled: "But as in the days (remember, part of the days of Noah were 'giant' filled days) of Noah were, so shall the coming of the Son of man be." (Matthew 24:37) Let us never forget that the days of the giants are not over yet. The world I believe has not seen the last giant!

3

HOW WERE GIANTS CREATED?
PART TWO

Genesis 6:4- There were **GIANTS** in the earth in those days; and also after that, when the sons of God came in unto the daughters of men, and they bare children to them, the same became mighty men which were of old, men of renown.

IN OUR LAST ARTICLE on 'giants' we discussed what I like to call 'the conservative view concerning the creation of giants'. In this chapter I would like to look at what I call 'the controversial view concerning the creation of giants'. The first teaching is simple: through the natural reproduction of the human race, a group of giant men were created through genetics which would eventually so corrupt the world that God had to destroy them by a flood (Genesis 6:4–7)! In the second interruption that has come down through the history of the Bible, we have a different teaching on just who 'the sons of God' were and who 'the daughters of men' were. This is the controversial view: that the 'fallen ones' (nephilim) were fallen angels, and these demons had relationships with human women resulting in a race of gigantic men that were used to corrupt and control mankind.

The argument for this view runs something like this. Ever since Satan was thrown out of heaven, he had been looking for ways to get back at God and to defeat God's purpose of the Redeemer (Genesis 3:15) through a woman. His first, and we must say, successful attack was in the temptation of Adam and Eve in the Garden of Eden (Genesis 3). Despite the fact Satan didn't cause the fall of man (man did this on his own, don't ever use the argument that 'Satan made me do it' it won't hold up in God's court), he was nevertheless condemned for his part, as was the serpent, the man, the woman, and the ground (Genesis 3:14–19). The serpent's punishment was immediate (to forever crawl on its belly). Women would through child-bearing feel the wrath of God, and man through the sweat of his brow be reminded of his terrible choice. For Satan, all he heard was this: "And I will put enmity between thee and the woman, and between THY SEED and her seed; it shall bruise thy head, and thou shalt bruise HIS HEEL (Jesus death on Calvary-just a bruise because His was not fatal because He rose again)." (Genesis 3:15) Satan at this time didn't know everything of what this condemnation meant, but he was smart enough to know that when his punishment came it would come through a woman, not a man. It was then I believe Satan hatched his demonic plan to corrupt 'the seed of the woman' and create his own 'seed' (giants) using the angels that fell with him!

When Satan was cast out of Heaven (Luke 10:18), he didn't fall alone. Two Biblical authors speak about Satan's companions in wickedness: **"For if God spared not the angels that sinned, but cast them down to hell, and delivered them into chains of darkness, to be reserved unto judgment,"** (II Peter 2:4) and **"And the angels which kept no their first estate, but left their own habitation, he hath reserved in everlasting chains under darkness unto the judgment of the great day."** (Jude 6). How many of the heavenly host, angelic host fell with Satan is given to us in Revelation 12:4: "And his tail drew _**the third part**_ of the stars of heaven, and did cast them to the earth...." If you read on in Revelation 12:7–9 you will link the fall of Satan with the fall of a third of the angels of heaven: Satan's seed, or was there to be another seed?

We can also discover from the Scriptures that the phrase: 'the sons of God' can be associated with angels. Read carefully Job 1:6, Job 2:1, and Job 38:7! Granted, it is used to also speak about normal human beings as well (John 1:12), but in the argument of the corrupting of **'the seed of the wom-an'**, some of these fallen angels had intercourse with some women resulting in a supernatural conception that created a race of monstrosities called in the Bible 'giants'. Remember, the basic meaning of the word translated 'gi-ant' is NEPHILIM, or 'fallen ones'. Some interpret the phrase in Jude 6: **'first estate'** as not speaking of the abode of heaven, but the sexless creature we call angel (Matthew 22:29–30). When angels are mentioned in the Bible they are portrayed as sexless and always in the male gender, but nowhere can we find it said they couldn't have sex? Were Peter and Jude referring to just the angels that fell with Satan from the portals of Heaven, or were they referring to a group of those fallen angels that went a step to far for God's liking and did something that brought on an instant confinement?

We know that Satan himself is loose on this planet to this day (Ephesians 2:2), he is not confined as of yet (Revelation 20:1–3). We know that he has at his disposal a group of angles called demons, also free. There are numerous stories in the Gospels about Jesus confronting demons seemingly free to move about (Matthew 8:28–34), yet, the angels described by Peter in II Peter 2:4 and Jude in Jude 6 seem to be already in come kind of prison; confinement for a crime above and beyond their original sin of rebelling against the Almighty in heaven itself (Isaiah 14 and Ezekiel 28). Could that sin be the part they played in corrupting the human race before the Flood? Interestingly, the Septuagint, the translation of the Old Testament from Hebrew to Greek in 280 BC, translates 'sons' as 'angels'. The great Jewish historian Josephus held to this doctrine of the creation of 'giants'. Justin Martyr who lived between 110 and 165 AD believed in this concept of 'giants'. Martin Luther taught that it was the fornication of angels with women that resulted in the evil race (Satan's seed) known as 'giants', and you have probably figured out by now that I have become fully persuaded in my own mind that this is the right Biblical interruption (Romans 14:5).

There does seem to be enough Scriptural evidence to teach that there are two distinct angelic groups of fallen angels: those still free with Satan roaming (I Peter 5:8) on the earth causing havoc like they did with Job (Job 1–2) and a group of angels already imprisoned waiting the final judgment (Revelation 9:14–21). Two categories of demons, why? What was it that caused God to put a selected group of fallen angels away? I have always gotten great insight into demonology in the story of the demonic of the Gergesenes. Remember when Jesus confronted them they cried, "What have we to do with Thee, Jesus, Thou Son of God? Art Thou come hither to torment us before the time?" (Matthew 8:29) They knew Jesus and they knew He would be their judge at the judgment and they knew that their destiny was a place of torment (the lake of fire), but they were surprised that it might be then. Another illustration into the falsehood that Satan or any of his demons are all-knowing, or know God's times! You know the rest of the story: Jesus allowing them to go freely into the swine because their time of ultimate imprisonment wasn't yet.

As with the conservative view, this controversial view leaves us with many questions, like, how do sexless, spiritual creatures have intercourse with women? How would God allow such a sacrilege in the first place when He would have known the spiritual ramifications to the human race? And how do you kill with water an angel or the offspring of an angel? I will leave you to decide. As for me, despite some unanswered questions, I believe it is the only interpretation that helps to understand the role 'giants' play throughout the rest of their history in the Bible. We can't ignore them, so we must deal with him according to our best understanding of their creation, or formation?

4

AND ALSO AFTER THAT
GIANTS

Genesis 6:4-There were **GIANTS** in the earth in those days; **AND ALSO AFTER THAT**, when the sons of God came in unto the daughters of men, and they bare children to them, the same became mighty men which were of old, men of renown.

IT IS TIME WE try to connect the 'giants' before the Flood to the 'giants' after the Flood. Moses, the human author of the books from Genesis to Deuteronomy, is our only link between these two very different periods in earth's history; made much different by the universal Flood. As Moses was describing the birth of the 'giants' in Genesis 6:4, he was also confronting 'giants' as he lead the children of Israel from Egypt to Canaan by way of the exodus. Only twice is the Hebrew word 'nephilim' (giants) used in the Hebrew text. Moses is the only author of the Bible that uses that word. In its first use in Genesis 6:4, Moses is referring to the antediluvian 'giants', but in Numbers 13:33 he is making reference to the Canaanite 'giants' the spies encountered on their exploratory trip into the highlands of the Promised Land. In Moses' use of the same word, he is in my opinion telling us that there is a link between the 'giants' of these widely separated 'giant' groups. It was that belief in their connection that caused Moses to write under the in-spiration of the Holy Spirit (II Peter 1:21): **"....and also after that...."** It will be through the writings of Moses that we will be able to link the pre-flood 'giants' with the most famous race of 'giants' in the Bible: the Anakims of Numbers 13:33.

Depending on your understanding of how 'giants' were created will determine how you connect the antediluvian 'giants' with their post-flood cousins. If you are one that believers in the human creation of 'giants' then you would say the race of 'giants' after the flood came through Noah's son Ham (Genesis 14:5-more on this connection in our next article). If you on the other hand believe in the demonic creation of 'giants' then you would say that Satan simply resurrected an old 'device' (II Corinthians 2:11) to help him resist the plan of God to strike at him through the woman (Genesis 3:15), to once and for all block the predicted head wound to him by the Person of Christ. If there was no occupation of the Promised Land by the people of God then the Christ couldn't be born! For whichever interpretation you adhere to will still require you to explain how the 'giants' managed to pass through the destructive waters of the world-wide Flood?

Moses remains silent about the existence of 'giants' from Genesis 6 until Genesis 14. Then he goes silent again until Numbers and then Deuteronomy. The first thought that came to me is that Moses himself never placed much value in the 'giants'; certainly they existed but were insignificant in the mind of Moses. They might be interesting and fascinating to some, but Moses actual only mentions them EIGHT times in his five books. For me this speaks volumes about the importance Moses put on this diabolical device of the Devil. They might have been powerful, mighty, strong, tall, but the reality of these abnormally large men is the simple fact they were just that: men. And Moses had the Almighty God on his side. In the writings of Moses, this was just another story of man verses God; granted, mighty men verses the Almighty God, but nothing more. A superhuman race of men, dinosaur-men, maybe, but just men! An old preacher friend of mine uses to say, **"The best of men are just men at best!"** Could I say this, the biggest of men are just men at best when compared to God, for even a titan is a pigmy when sized up against the eternal God.

If there were dinosaurs on the ark, I believe the DNA to create a super race of people was also on that ark. As we have learned, the nature of depravity that eventually destroyed the antediluvian world was also on Noah's boat. Within the heart of those eight human beings was carried all the wickedness , unrighteousness, and vileness that could and would come out of mankind after the Flood; just as it was seen before the Flood. Within a very short time after their disembarking, the family of Noah was revealing its bend to sin in the story of Noah and his son Ham (Genesis 9:20–24). Is the answer to our $64,000 question as simple as the 'giants' escaping annihilation by way of the ark? Or did the 'giants' escape destruction by way of Satan; spirits can't be destroyed by water (Remember the story of the demons and the swine-Mark 5:12–13)! Until Satan was convinced his grand creation of a race of super soldiers wouldn't stop the plans of God; he would reassign them to places where either God or the people of God would have to confront them. Before we go on to acknowledge the first named 'giant', I would have you consider that connection to Satan and his super soldiers.

The first sign that a race or a number of races of 'giants' came out of Noah's family is mentioned in Genesis 14:5. In our next chapter, I will write more on the Rephaims, the Zuzims, and the Emims. As for now, I have found another interesting connection between the first named giant: Rephaim (Genesis 15:20). There is a Hebrew word RAPHA which is translated 'giant' in six places in II Samuel 21 and I Chronicles 20 (more about this Rapha later), but there are some who make the link between Rapha and Rephaim. Rapha means 'fearful ones'; this characteristic above and beyond any other quality of 'giant' is forever linked to Biblical 'giants'. It would be the fear of 'giants' that would keep the children of Israel out of Canaan for 40 years (Numbers 13:33). It would be the fear of Goliath that would keep the soldiers of King Saul's army at bay for 40 days (I Samuel 17:16). The giant 'fear' is still one of the Devil's best and most often used tactics against God's people. I have taught for years that it isn't death that the Devil controls, but **'the fear of death'** he uses against us: "Forasmuch then as the children are partakers of flesh and blood, he also himself likewise took part of the same; that through death he might destroy him that had the power of death, that is, the devil; and deliver them who through **fear of death** were all their lifetime subject to bondage." (Hebrews 2:14–15)

I guess what I am trying to get across to you in this chapter is that our archenemy hasn't really given up on a favorite device. What he has learned over the millennium is to repackage his devices into different forms and shapes. The fear of 'giants' was all he needed to bring the world into his fold whether in the pre-Flood world or the post-Flood world. Giants were used to bring God's people under the bondage of fear; that is until men like Moses and David and others lost their fear of 'giants'. Let us not forget the teaching of Jesus: "And fear not them (including giants) which kill the body, but rather fear Him which is able to destroy the soul and body in hell." (Matthew 10:28) It is amazing to me that the very enemy we fight against knows this lesson better than we do: "Thou believest that there is one God; thou doest well: the devils also believe, and tremble (fear)!" (James 2:19) It is time we learn that the device of the Devil we should not be ignorant of is 'fear'! We should also learn that faith has always defeated fear. When faith replaces fear, fear must flee, just like Satan must flee (James 4:7) Only when we realize that fear is all bark and no bite will we like Moses recognize fears limitations!

So who was Satan's Super Solider named Rephaim, and what was his demonic assignment in the ongoing battle against God and God's people?

5

REPHAIM
THE FIRST GIANT

Genesis 14:5-And in the fourteenth year came Chedorlaomer, and the kings that were with him, and smote the **REPHAIMS** in Ashteroth Karnaim, and the Zuzims in Ham, and the Eminms in Shaveh Kiriathaim.

WITH SATAN'S FIRST 'GIANTS' (Genesis 6:4) being wiped out in the universal Flood, the Devil was not quite ready to give up on this device of diabolical corruption. The original 'giants' had helped Lucifer destroy (Genesis 6:5) the entire human race except for 'eight' (I Peter 3:20), so he reasoned they might be able to help him against Noah's Race, or were they already in Noah's race? Note, the mention of a place called Ham in our key verse printed above, could this be named after Noah's second son (Genesis 5:32)?

The first Biblical named 'giant' was Rephaim, or 'strong or lofty man'! That name would be given to a race of 'giants' that lived just south of Jerusalem. Satan is not all-knowing, but he is not stupid either! Satan never forgot what he had learned in heaven, and I believe he came to understand the importance of Jerusalem in the eternal plan of God. Note, by the time of the history recorded in Genesis 14 Salem was occupied by a priest/king named Melchizedek and Paul would tell us in Hebrews 7 that was the incarnate Christ! So it was not by chance or circumstance that Satan placed his first 'giants' after the Flood near Jerusalem! Interestingly, a valley would eventually be named after Rephaim (the valley of giants) located southwest of Jerusalem and just north of Bethlehem. I had a chance to travel through that valley in my 2010 trip to Israel. It is called El Bukaa today; but then, the Promised Land was settled by the Jews, and this valley would become the border between the Tribe of Judah and the Tribe of Benjamin (Joshua 15:8, II Samuel 5:18, 22, I Chronicles 11:15, 14:9, and Isaiah 17:5). Satan didn't know the timing of all of God's moves, but he had his 'giants' in place when Abraham first entered the land of promise. I have come to believe that the 'giants' (note the plural because there was more than one group) were positioned to block God's occupation of the strategic mountaintop position eventually called Jerusalem. (II Samuel 5: 6–9)

All we know about these early post-flood 'giants' is what we can glean from their names. In what I believe was a preemptive strike by God against Satan's super soldiers, Rephaims' races were attacked by a confederacy of kings lead by Chedorlaomer, the king of Elam. On his way to deal with a revolt by the five city-states of Sodom, Gomorrah, Adamah, Zebolim, and Bela (Genesis 14:1–4), Chedorlaomer had to pass through the lands of the 'giants'. They resisted and were defeated one by one. There is no evidence that Chedorlaomer had any 'giants' in his army, yet the famous 'mighty men' of Rephaim were no match against the soldiers of Shinar (Babylon), Ellasar, Elam, and the warriors of the King Tidal, the king of nations. I feel the precept of Proverbs 21:1 is being illustrated in this historical military campaign: **"The king's heart is in the hand of the Lord, as the rivers of water: He turneth it whithersoever He will!"**

Chedorlaomer first smote the Rephaims in their capital of Ashteroth Karnaim (Genesis 14:5): meaning 'the two-horned Ashtaroth'. The site of this city is located in the highlands of Bashan on the east bank of the Jordan River. (We will see another named giant, OG, come out of Bashan later on in our study.) Seemingly, the race of Rephaims had settled on both banks of the Jordan? Then Chedorlaomer took out the Zuzims in Ham (Genesis 14:5). Zuzim means 'tall ones'. They occupied the table land south of Bashan and Gilead. We will see them again in Deuteronomy 2:20 as Zamzummim. Little is known of the location of their capital at Ham. Was this the link to the 'giants' and Noah's son? We should never forget the powerful prophecy of Noah and the Biblical curse placed in Ham. (Read carefully Genesis 9:20–29.) Did God know beforehand what would come out of Canaan? He certainly did and could one of those curses be upon the races of 'giants' found in that land in the days of Abraham; devilish 'giants, demonic titans, and diabolical gargantuans of a group of races?

After defeating the Rephaims and the Zuzims (note they were defeated not wiped-out), Chedorlaomer took on the Emims in Shaveh Kiriathaim (Genesis 14:5): 'the dale of the two cities'. Emim means 'terrible ones': as we have seen lofty ones, tall ones, terrible ones, and feared ones! The Emims were located just south of the Zuzims directly east of the Dead Sea. Eventually their land would be occupied by the Moabites. If we continue our trace of the nations defeated by Chedorlaomer army, we discover that the route they took to punish the city-states of the plain was the famous trade route called 'the King's Highway'. This ancient trek followed the east bank of the Jordan River all the way from Damascus in the north, around the southern tip of the Dead Sea, and on to Egypt.

Ultimately, Chedorlaomer would defeat the five kings of the south at the Battle of the Valley of Siddim (Salt) (Genesis 14:8–12). Most ancient history scholars believe the war was over the original Middle East 'oil': Salt! Chedorlaomer only military mistake in his western campaign was his capture of the people of Sodom. Unknown to him he sweep up the family of Lot in his spoils which brought Abram and Abram's God into the story (Genesis 14:13–16). In an amazing feat of strategy Abram armed his own household (only 318 against the combined armies of four powerful eastern countries) and marched after this vast army, and just southwest of Damascus at a place called Dan (Genesis 14:14) he defeated this professional army in a surprise night attack and recaptured his nephew Lot. It is here I believe that Abram had an encounter with the Devils 'giants'!

If Chedorlaomer took Lot captive; you can't tell me that he didn't also take a few 'giants' home as trophies of war. To 'lead captivity captive' was an old tradition of ancient warriors to show just how successful a military campaign had been. It was not unheard of to bring captive soldiers into one's own army after a battle, especially if those warriors were paid as mercenaries. So at the Battle of Dan when Abram divided his forces and took on the military might of Elam, were there 'giants' there? Could Abram be considered one of the 'first' giant-killers of the Bible? Rephaim had long since died, but the race of gigantic men that came out of him where still alive. Despite being outnumbered (thousands against hundreds), outclassed (professionals against amateurs), outmatched (soldiers against shepherds-sound familiar), and under-sized (giants verses men), the victory went to God's man and His men.

We will see this result again and again as we work our way through the Biblical text confronting Satan's super soldiers. Each and every time they are stood up to by God's man they are ultimately the ones outnumbered like in the day of Elijah (II Kings 6:17), overmatched because **"If God be for us, who can be against us?"** (Romans 8:31) This precept by Paul also includes encounters with 'giants'! The size of your features isn't what counts, but the size of your faith in the Almighty God. That is all that really matters when you're face to face with a giant. Whether or not Abraham actually battled 'giants' or not I can't be dogmatic, but my personal opinion is that he did, but the lesson is clearly seen in the campaign of Chedorlaomer: mere men with God's help are better than Satan's 'giants' in any battle!

6

THE GIANTS CALLED
REPHAIMS

Genesis 15:20-And the Hittites, and the Perizzites, and the **REPHAIMS**.

THE ABRAHAMIC COVENANT (GENESIS 15:18) included among such things to Abram's descendants as **'a promised land'**. 'This Land' engulfed all the territory between the River of Egypt (Nile or a Wadi in the Sinai?) and the River Euphrates. This was not an uninhabited land (still the big controversy in the Middle East today between the Jews and the Palestinians), but a land of at least ten distinct people groups (Genesis 15:19–21). As Abraham, Isaac, and Jacob sojourned (Hebrews 11:9) in 'this land' (Genesis 14:14–17), they came into contact with the various races of Canaan, including the Rephaims: the giants. God had promised Abraham that his descendants would one day replace the giants of Canaan!

In A. R. Fausset's Bible Dictionary, he gives this definition of the Rephaims:

> "Rephaims: a people defeated by Chedorlaomer at Ashteroth Karnaim (Genesis 14:5), occupying the northeast of the Jordan Valley (Peraea) before the Canaanites came. OG, the giant king of Bashan, was the last of them (Deuteronomy 3:11). They once extended to the southwest, for the valley of Rephaim was near the valley of Hinnom and Bethlehem, just south of Jerusalem, _'the valley of giants'_ (Joshua 15:8, 18:16, II Samuel 5:18, 22, 23:13).

Rephaim was used for 'the dead', or their ghosts (Job 27:6-the souls of the dead tremble); Psalm 88:10, Proverbs 2; 18, 9:18, and Isaiah 14:9, 26:19; perhaps, because Sheol, or Hades was thought to be the abode of the buried giants!"

In our quest to discover a link between Satan and the 'giants', perhaps, this is our second piece of evidence. Our first link, you remember, was the teaching that the original 'giants' of Genesis 6:4 came from the angels that fell with Satan. So we have a connection with Lucifer in Isaiah 14:12–15. This passage of Scripture describes the fall of God's first created being. Compare verse 15 and verse 9 of Isaiah 14 and the final abode of Lucifer is linked to the name Rephaim. Put together and I conclude that the 'giants' were a product of Lucifer: the first 'giant': a being that saw himself bigger than life, bigger than God! I also draw from the meaning of Rephaim that these 'giants' were so fearful that the memory of them was like 'a ghost story' to those who had seen one. They were your nightmare, the boogie man in your campfire tale. Even in death they brought a great foreboding whenever there name was mentioned (we will deal with this aspect of 'giants' when we study the life of the last Rephaim: the super-sized giant called OG). I am convinced that there is a link between the destination of the dead giants and this teaching of Jesus: "Then shall he say also unto them on the left hand, Depart from me, ye cursed, into everlasting fire, PREPARED FOR THE DEVIL AND HIS ANGELS." (Matthew 25:41) The abode of the Devil and his demons and his 'giants' is the same!

Fausset goes on to explain the other two giant races connected to the Rephaims, the Emims and the Zuzims we saw in our last chapter:
"Emims: terror; so called for their terrible stature by the Moabites, who succeeded them in the region east of the Jordan (Deuteronomy 2:10). Or rather the word the Egyptians term Amu, nomad Shemites. This race was also smitten by Chedorlaomer at Shaveh Kiriathaim (Genesis 14:5). (Fausset also thinks there is a link between the Emims and the Anakims: more later.) The Zuzims of Ham were a northern tribe of Rephaim between the Arnon and Jabbok rivers, smitten by Chedorlaomer (Genesis 14:50. The Ammonites who supplanted them called them Zamzummim (Deuteronomy 2:20). Connected with the Horim, Le Clerc explains the name 'wanderers' from "zuz": 'to wander'. Ham maybe the origin of the site called Rabbath Ammon. The ruined cities of Bashan are thought by many to evidence their possession formerly by giant races. The success of David and his heroes against Goliath and the 'giants' of Philistia (a remnant of the

old giant races) illustrates the Divine principle that physical might and size are nothing worthy, nay, are but beast-strength, when severed from God and arrayed against the people of God. Samson was but of average height (Judges 16:17), yet was irresistible by the Philistines so long as he was faithful to God. David was chosen above his brothers in spite of their 'height of stature' (I Samuel 16:7, 17:36–37, 45–47 and II Samuel 21:15–22)."
Maybe, we have come to another one of the great principles of God that must be gleaned when you study Biblical; giants'! Did the 'giants' have any hope when going up against 'a man of God'?

Despite their superior height and exceptional strength (remember, one of the meanings of Rephaim is 'strong'), the Rephaims were no match seemingly to anybody; God's men or mortal man, the godly or the ungodly. Chedorlaomer was not a man of God nor was his army, but they were simply men used by God to punish the wicked. Paul described this precept best when he wrote these words in a letter to the Christians of Corinth: "For you see your calling, brethren, how that not many wise after the flesh, not many mighty (giants), not many noble, are called: but God hath chosen the foolish things of the world to confound the wise; and the weak things (a young shepherd boy) of the world to confound the things which are mighty (Goliath); and the base things of the world, and the things which are despised, hath God chosen, yea, and the things that are not, to bring to nought things that are: that no flesh should glory in His presence." (I Corinthians 1:26–29) Giants were all about self-glorification or the glorification of the Devil. Satan's strategy was destined to fail from the very beginning because his diabolical device was created directly against a core tenet of God Holy Word: 'that no flesh (even giant flesh) should glory in His presence'!

Ponder with me for a few final moments the application of the Rephaims to this precept explained by Paul. There were probably no people stronger than the Rephaims. There was probably no group of people mightier than the Rephaims. In our study of the last of the Rephaims, we will come face to face with the biggest giant recorded in the Bible; yes, bigger than Goliath! Why then did the giants fall? Because they placed themselves directly in the path of God's divine purpose. Their glory was in their size, height, power. As with today, many see their glory in their body, belly, or biceps. I believe the 'giants' were ugly, not beautiful. They sought the fear factor not the appeal factor. Beauty is today the new giant; outward appearance is the new god, the new giant. Is it not for this reason that God chose a boy to defeat a giant; ordinary nobodies to defeat the undefeatable (wait till you meet the giant-killers of the Bible, I guarantee you will not have heard of many of them-no Samson included), the invalid taking on the invincible? Satan created 'giants' as an instrument of his power and strength, but like all his other devices the 'giant' proved to be powerless against God and His instruments. Let us highlight and underline and never forget this marvellous promise given to us thought the pen of the prophet Isaiah: **"No weapon that is formed against thee shall prosper...."** (Isaiah 54:17) I believe that included the weapon called 'giant'. When God put the Rephaims on His 'hit list' in the days of Abraham, every 'giant' was already doomed, destined to destruction from that day forward. Oh, they would survive for a few hundred years or more, but one by one they would go down to defeat until there was only one Rephaim left!

7

THE VALLEY OF THE GIANTS

Joshua 15:8-And the border went up by the valley of the son of Hinnom unto the south side of Jebusite; the same is Jerusalem: and the border went up to the top of the mountain that lieth before the valley of Hinnom westward, which is at the end of **THE VALLEY OF GIANTS** northward.

So whatever happened to the Rephaims?

The first homeland of the Rephaims (Emims and Zuzims included) seemingly was on the east bank of the Jordan. We have come to this conclusion because of the information gleaned from Genesis 14 and the first recorded war in that region with the conquest of Chedorlaomer's army in their lands. It seems to me that they might have been defeated and displaced, but some survived! When the Rephaims, Emims, and Zuzims were scattered, where did they go?

In the Biblical accounts of events, sometimes, it is the places, not the people we need to keep an eye on. I have for many years been a student of Biblical geography. As I write this book on Satan's Super Soldiers, I am conducting my 43rd evening school class. Since 1979, I have been having what I like to call 'Winter in the Word' classes (at the compiling of these series of articles on 'giants' in book form I am into my 44th year of evening school conducting my 51th class with my latest course: Jerusalem: its history, geography, and prophecy. These in-depth Bible studies have been held at my last three pastorates. The classes have averaged about 26 weeks usually starting in September and concluding in April. These studies have been held on Tuesday night and have been about an hour or so in length. For nearly a decade I offered a choice of two classes each Tuesday night, but after my first ten years I have only taught one class per season. This year's winter topic is "The Geography of the Early Church": a study in the journeys of Peter and Paul. Actually this course is the last in a four part series on Biblical geography. I have two Old Testament courses: "The Journey of God's People from Adam to Moses" and "The Journey of God's People from Joshua to the Kings". I have also compiled two New Testament classes: "The Journey of Jesus in the Gospels" and 'The Journey of Peter and Paul in the Acts". And there is only one way to answer the question that begins this chapter on Biblical 'giants': geography!

The only mention of Rephaim (except for the giant OG-more later) is the valley that bears his name. Located on the west bank of the Jordan River, I have come to the belief that the remnant of the Rephaims escaped over the Jordan and re-established themselves in the valley that would be the future borderland of the tribe of Judah and the tribe of Benjamin (the verse printed above is the description of that boundary). There is no indication that any of the Rephaims were there at the time of the conquest of the region by Joshua and the armies of Israel, for they had seemingly been replaced by the Canaanites, but that doesn't mean that their legacy didn't linger on, for whoever journeyed into that valley knew they were walking through the land of the 'giants'. Years later, the Hebrew historian who recorded the life of Israel in Canaan wanted us to know of 'the valley of the giants'. In my travels through Israel in 2010, I was able to pass through this valley several times as we explored the territory around Jerusalem, and to this day it is still being referred to as 'the valley of the giants' by the tour guides!

The best explanation of this valley I have found is recorded by Andrew Robert Fausset, famous for his co-authoring of a commentary on the whole Bible by Jamieson, Fausset, and Brown. Fausset complied his Bible dictionary at Saint Cuthbert's Rectory in York, England in the 1940s. He writes this on the history of 'the valley of Rephaim':

"II Samuel 5:18, 5:22, 23:13; I Chronicles 11:15, 14:9; and Isaiah 17:5. In Joshua 15:8, it is translated 'the valley of giants'. The scene of David's twice routing the Philistines utterly and destroying their idols; so that it was named Perazim, God breaking forth upon David's foes (for they came to seek him to avenge their old quarrel, on hearing of his accession to the throne of Israel); a type of God's future utter overthrow of the Church's last foes (Isaiah 38:21–22). The Philistines came in harvest time to the valley, to carry off the ripe crops in II Samuel 23:13, Isaiah 17:5. Joshua (15:8) says Judah's boundary 'went up to the top of the mountain that lieth before the valley of Hinnom westward, which is at the end of the valley of Rephaim (giants) northward.' The most northern point of the Valley of Rephaim was at the summit that terminated the valley of Hinnom on the west. Its proximity to Bethlehem is implied in II Samuel 23:13–17. Bethlehem was south of Jerusalem. Moreover, the Philistines' natural line of march to Jerusalem would be from the southwest. Hence it likely the valley of Rephaim is the wide elevated plain which, beginning at the top of the valley of Hinnom, stretches south along the road to Bethlehem, but gradually bends west until it contracts into the narrow, deep valley (wady el werd)!"

The day our study group from Dallas Theological Seminary travelled to Bethlehem we drove through this valley of the 'giants', the Rephaim. The old 'giants' are gone, but their valley remains as it was when they stocked the land and scared the people of God. The only 'giants' left are the terrorist that are doing the same thing today!

The race we call the Rephaims settled in this valley during the days of Abraham. Called the valley of Elbukaa today, this is a natural placement for Satan's Super Soldiers at a very strategic place between two very important locations in Biblical history: Bethlehem and Jerusalem. I do not believe it was by mere chance or circumstance that the remnant of Rephaim found a refuge in this valley. If we watch the contest, the chess match between the good verses the bad, right verses wrong unfold in the Scriptures: the titanic struggle between Satan and Jehovah, it was nothing more than a series of checks and counter movements between the two ancient adversaries. Satan getting his people into Canaan first, then God moving his people (Abraham) in, while chasing the giants around with other people groups (Chedorlaomer) from the east. Once God's intent was clear; once Satan knew that God had promised Abraham's descendants the land, Satan started to settle his super soldiers in the heart of the land to defend it from occupation by the people group (Jews) that would bring about Satan's ultimate defeat by the hand of the Messiah. As we saw in our last chapter, ten pagan races (Genesis 15:19–21) were positioned to resist God's divine plan of redemption, and included in their number were a collection of super races of 'giants'!

So it will be for us in our lives. Satan will strategically place certain people in the places of our lives to disrupt our faith, to detour our walk, to distract our focus, and if possible to defeat us enough so we will get discouraged in the work of the Lord. Satan knows he can't ultimately recapture us (II Timothy 2:26), but he can harass us and hound us, and haunt us to the point we might just give up the fight; that we might fall away (I Timothy 4:1). We will be fighting 'giants' to the end of our days in 'the valley of giants' called 'this world', but we can be 'more than conquers' with Christ. (Romans 8:37)

8

OG
THE FINAL REPHAIM

Deuteronomy 3:11-For **OG** king of Bashan remained of **THE REMNANT OF GIANTS**; behold, his bedstead was a bedstead of iron; is it not in Rabbath of the children of Ammon? Nine cubits was the length thereof, and four cubits the breadth of it, after the cubit of a man. (a measurement from the tip of the middle finger to the elbow)

WHEN SHALL WE EVER learn that **'bigger isn't always better'**? (The Titanic comes to mind!) In the Word of God BIG is often an instrument of the Devil rather than a method use by God. The Hebrew prophet Zechariah questions: **"For who hath despised the day of small things?"** (Zechariah 4:10) Some of the most unique stories of Scripture revolve around Satan's use of 'giants' against God's people. The primary reason given for why the ten spies of Israel thought their nation could never conquer Canaan was "And there we saw the 'giants', the sons of Anak which came of the 'giants', and we were in our own sight as grasshoppers, and so we were in their sight." (Numbers 13:33) At the time of the Exodus the Promised Land was infested with gigantic human beings planted there. We have learned planted by Satan to defend the land from the onslaught of God's army and to defeat God's plan of redemption of mankind through the Jewish people. Though this titanic fear worked on the first generation of Hebrews out of Egypt, eventually these 'giants' proved no match for God's smaller, but faithful men.

Goliath of Gath is perhaps the most famous giant of the Bible, but he is certainly not the only giant of the Bible. Goliath's defeat at the hands of a young shepherd boy from Bethlehem is one of the most recognized events of Holy Writ (I Samuel 17-more later). But David was not the only giant-killer! Benaiah, one of David's mighty men, is recorded to have slain an Egyptian giant (II Samuel 23:21). Abishai, David's cousin, killed a giant named Ishbibenob as he was about ready to kill David when David was nearly 60 years of age (II Samuel 21:15–17). At the Battle of Gob, Sibbechai, another one of David's mighty men, destroyed the giant Saph (II Samuel 21:18). The giant Lahmi, one of Goliath's brothers, was defeated and killed by another one of David's trusted soldiers by the name of Elhanan (I Chronicles 20:5). Then David's nephew Jonathan, the son of David's brother Shimea, killed a six-finger giant at the Battle of Gath (II Samuel 21:20–21). But what of the greatest giant of them all: OG? I have come to believe in my study of Biblical 'giants' that OG was Satan's biggest giant in Palestine; yes, bigger, wider, taller, heavier than Goliath! Yet in the Battle for Canaan, despite OG's strength, size, weight, he too was defeated by God's warriors, and though I don't believe they face each other, I do believe that Moses was ultimately the victor over the giant OG.

When the Israelites were forced to invade Canaan from the east, one of the kingdoms they had to conquer on the east bank of the Jordan was the Kingdom of Bashan; a kingdom ruled by the giant called OG. OG was an Ammonite king whose kingdom included sixty city-states in the Transjordan. His strongholds included the important cities of Edrei and Ashtaroth (Joshua 13:12 and Joshua 12:4). OG could trace his descendants back to the days of Abraham (Genesis 14:5), but in his day, he was considered the last of his branch of the giant races (Deuteronomy 3:11). After Moses' armies, under the generalship of Joshua, captured the territory of Sihon they marched on Bashan, and in the decisive Battle of Edrei, OG and his people were wiped out (Numbers 21:33–35). However, the uniqueness of the victory over the giant OG lived on, far into the future. Twenty-two times the defeat of OG is mentioned in the Scriptures. Years later the Psalmist was still singing of the death of OG (Psalm 135:11, 136:20). When Nehemiah reminded the people of the Babylonian Captivity of their past, one of the events he retold was Israel's victory over OG (Nehemiah 9:22). What made

OG's defeat so famous, or infamous? I believe it had to do with OG's mammoth size!

In all the references to OG, there is only one verse that gives a hint to his actual size. I gave you the King James Version to start this chapter, but let me now give you the New International version: "Only OG king of Bashan was left of the remnant of the Rephaims. His bed was made of iron and was more than 13 feet long and 6 feet wide. It is still in Rabbath of the Ammonites." (Deuteronomy 3:11 NIV) Many that have studied this text have come to believe this verse describes OG's bier, or sarcophagus (his coffin). Whether his literal bed (a single bed at that), or his death bed; for Moses, this gigantic bed was worth noting in the divine text! It seems the question of the KJV: "Is it not in Rabbath of the children of Ammon?" is a suggestion that OG's bed had become a kind of a tourist attraction. Was the bed in a kind of museum? Or was the sarcophagus in the open, a memorial tomb, like Alexander the Great's bier in Alexandria, Egypt? How big would a man have to be to have a bed or a coffin that huge? Big! And the noting that the bed was made of iron suggests to me the weight of this giant was so great that wood would not due in the construction of his sleeping place!

Despite OG's size his end had been sealed when the Lord God of Israel said: "Fear him (OG) not for I have delivered him (OG) into thy hand." (Numbers 21:34) Satan's 'giants' were no match for Moses, Joshua, or Caleb (Joshua 14-more later). Each giant in his time would be faced down by a giant-killer. That is why, in my opinion, the defeat of OG was mentioned so many times in the Hebrew text; to encourage those who still had 'giants' to face! Life can produce 'giants' in every generation. As they tower above us we feel helpless and the battle seems hopeless, but God would have us know through His Word that with His help we are better than any giant Satan can put on the field of battle. John Bunyan wrote of the Giant Despair in his classic work: Pilgrim's Progress. And though his hero Christian was imprisoned by Giant Despair for a season (like the Israelite of the Exodus), he too eventually escaped from his gigantic foe. Many years ago a favorite hymn writer, Philip Bliss, wrote a song he titled: Dare to be a Daniel; in the third stanza he penned: "Many giants' great and tall, staking through the land, head long to the earth would fall if meet by Daniel's band. Dare to be a Daniel, dare to stand alone, dare to have a purpose form, dare to make it known." (Why Daniel instead of David?)

It doesn't say that OG was defeated singlehandedly, but nearly all of the other 'giants' of the Bible were, so why should this be an exception? All we have to do is dare to take a stand, to stand up to the 'giants' of our lives, and I believe the Lord will do the rest! Remember, **'the bigger they are the harder they fall!"** I don't know by what name your giant is called, but I do know that with the Lord's help you can defeat and destroy that giant, including the giant Lucifer (James 4:7). You might be as a 'grasshopper' in the giant's sight and in your sight, but your giant's destiny is the same as OG's was: a coffin with a tombstone that reads: "How the Mighty have Fallen!" (II Samuel 1:19) Let us remember this question by the Apostle John when we face our next giant: "Who is he that overcometh the world, but he that believeth that Jesus is the Son of God?" (I John 5:5) Sometimes it is Lucifer's giant we have to overcome. Overcoming is possible when we remember, "Greater is he that is in you, than he (giant) that is in the world!" (I John 4:4)

9

ARBA
THE FUTURE GIANT

Genesis 35:27-And Jacob came unto Isaac his father unto Mamre, unto **THE CITY OF ARBAH**, where Abraham and Isaac sojourned.

IN OUR SEARCH AND research for Satan's Super Soldiers in the Scriptures, we have come to the second major race of 'giants' mentioned in the Bible. The Rephaims were the first distinct tribe of 'giants' after the flood, but the Anakims hold the distinction of being the most feared of all the giant races; used by Lucifer to divert the children of God from occupying the future home of the Prince of Peace, the Messiah of the Jews, and the Saviour of the World: Jesus Christ!

As with Rephaim, so with Arba, we have very little information given in Holy Writ about the origin of this race of gigantic men. As with Rephaim, so with Arba, we know more of his descendants then we know about him, yet from the few references we have, we can piece together an explainable picture of this 'super-man' and the part he played in blocking the children of Israel from entering the Promised Land on their first attempt. In the words of W. E. Vine's "An Expository Dictionary of Old Testament Words" for 'giants', he describes what the Bible means when invoking the term 'anakim': "The Anakim (literally, 'long-necked' or 'strong-necked') are first mentioned as such in Deuteronomy 1:18. They were a race of 'giants' (Deuteronomy 2:10, 11); 'Rephaim', a word used to describe the early giant people

33

of Palestine. In Numbers 13:33, they are spoken of as 'the nephilim (giant), the sons of Anak, which came of the Nephilim (giants).' Anak is thus regarded as the ancestor. The word 'Anak', however, may be the name of the race rather than an individual. This is indicated by the use of the article with the words ('the Anak') in the original in Numbers 13:33; Joshua 15:13, 14; Joshua 21:11; Judges 1:20. The greatest man among them was Arba, who gave his name to the city of Kirjath-ARBA, Joshua 14:15, but known better by the name Hebron, Genesis 23:2, 35:27. Arba seems to have been the progenitor of the race; presumably he founded the city of Hebron seven years before the Egyptian city of Zoan (Numbers 13:22)."

In Biblical history, the first to make contact with the Anakim was Abraham: "And Sarah died in Kirjath-ARBA; the same is Hebron in the land of Canaan...." (Genesis 23:2) As with his contact with the Rephaims in Genesis 14:5, I believe it was not by chance or happenstance or circumstance that Abraham crossed paths with the 'giants'. The 'giants' will be a thorn in the side of Abraham's descendants until the reign of David. In context, the death of Sarah, we gain our first bit of chronological evidence into the history of Arba: "And Abraham stood up from before his dead, and spake unto the sons of Heth...." (Genesis 23:3) Was Arba one of the sons of Heth? Were the Hethites the source of 'the long-necked ones'? Heth was the second son of Canaan, the son of Ham (Genesis 10:15 and I Chronicles 1:13). Is this another important piece of the gigantic puzzle that links the survival of the 'giants' after the Flood through Noah's son Ham and the races that come out of this man and his part in Satan's strategy?

Arba's call to Biblical fame was the building of one of the earliest (Jericho is considered the oldest but Hebron wasn't far behind) cities of Canaan: Kirjath-ARBA-the city of Arba. Vine suggest that the Anak was the race Arba fathered, but there are others that suggest that Anak was Arba's son because according to Numbers 13:22, Anak had three infamous giant sons who would resist Caleb's conquest of Hebron (more in another chapter). Or, as we saw with the Rephaims, were the sons of Anak just the giant races that came from Arba: Sheshai, Ahiman, and Talmai? Whichever history theory is correct, the bottom line is that unlike the Rephaims, the Anakims survived in numbers (remember, only one Rephaim survived long enough to oppose Israel's move into Canaan-the giant Og) to oppose the children of Abraham. As I have highlighted and underlined before, and we will certainly underline and highlight again; the primary reason for the first generation of Jews out of Egypt not gaining access to Canaan from their southern approach through Kadesh-Barnea was because of their fear of the Anakims: "But the men (the famous 12 spies) that went up with him (Caleb), said, we be not able to go up against the people; for they are stronger ('strong-necked') than we. And they brought up an evil report of the land which they had searched unto the children of Israel, saying, the land, through which we have gone to search it, is a land that eateth up the inhabitants thereof; and the people that we saw in it are men of great stature ('long-necked'). And there we saw the giants, the sons of Anak, which come of the giants: and we were in our own sight as grasshoppers, and so we were in their sight." (Numbers 13:31-33) If Rephaim was the first giant, then Arba was the future giant that would bring fear into the hearts and minds of the Israelites at the time of the Battle for Canaan!

Satan had planted his 'giants' in a very strategic spot to resist the invasion of Israel into Canaan. As I pondered this 'super-soldier', I was reminded that we can trace the roots of all our fears back to the Devil. Interestingly, Arba means: 'strength of Baal'. Baal was the primary god of the people of Canaan. Israel would struggle with Baalim throughout their history in Canaan. Think with me of the great contest between Elijah and the prophets of Baal on Mount Carmel (I Kings 18). I have come to believe that Baal worship was simply 'devil-worship' in disguise as are all false religion (check carefully-Deuteronomy 32:17 and Psalm 106:37). Satan has sought worship from his days in Heaven, and even from the Son of Man (Matthew 4:1-11). No wonder his chief agent in Canaan would be so named: 'the strength of Baal'-the strength of Satan?

We should never forget that our adversary can make himself into anything: "For such are....deceitful workers, transforming themselves.... And no marvel; for Satan himself is transformed into an angel of light. Therefore it is no great thing of his ministers also be transformed....whose end shall be according to their works." (II Corinthians 11:13-15) Satan and his 'super-soldiers' have always had the ability to make themselves into something they are not! Arba was the builder of a great and famous town, and little did Abraham know that the people he was dealing with at the time of his wife's death would produce a race of 'giants' that would nearly (note I said nearly not clearly) defeat his descendants. We too are in a great battle with a very dedicated and determined foe that will stop at nothing to prevent us from fulfilling God's divine plan and purpose for us. At first our enemies will seem civil and harmless as in the days of Abraham and Isaac, but in time they will grow into fearful foes as in the days of Joshua and

Caleb. They seek to scare us to death or frighten us always from our path; a characteristic of the Devil: "...the power of death that is the Devil; and delivers them who through fear of death were their entire lifetime subject to bondage." (Hebrews 2:14–15) Unless we simply trust in the directions of our Guide (even through giant infested lands), we too could be scared to death; immoveable, paralyzed in our tracks. 'Giants' can become obstacles only if we believe Satan's propaganda and his promotion and the picture he paints of the impossibility of defeating 'giants'. That is why we can never forget: "For with God nothing shall be impossible" (Luke 1:37) including defeating 'giants' in their own land!

10

A LAND OF GIANTS

Deuteronomy 2:20–21-(That also was accounted **A LAND OF GIANTS**: giants dwelt therein in old time; and the Ammonites called them Zamzummims; a people great and many, and tall, as the Anakims, but the Lord destroyed them before them, and they succeeded them, and dwelt in their stead.

As Israel worked its way around the tip of the Dead Sea, they came into 'a land of giants'. In our study of the giants of Abraham's day, we discovered that God was already destroying Satan's infestation of super soldiers. The first 'giant-killer' was God Himself. Three powerful, gigantic people groups were well established east of the Jordan by the time Jacob took his family to Egypt. Over the four hundred years Israel spent in Egypt; God began to systematically destroy these obstacles to the Hebrews return. Besides the verses we have printed above we need to add these to the record: "And the Lord said unto me, Distress not the Moabites, neither contends with them in battle: for I will not give thee their land for a possession; because I have given Ar unto the children of Lot for a possession. The Emims dwelt therein in times past, a people great, and many, and tall, as the Anakims; which also were accounted giants, as the Anakims; but the Moabites called them Emmims." (Deuteronomy 2:9–11)

What we have in Moses' journal in Deuteronomy chapter two is the history to the second generation of Israelites of just how Israel made their flanking attack into Canaan. Instead of attacking again from the south as their parents did (Numbers 14; 40–45), the leadership of Moses, Aaron,

Joshua, and Caleb had led the armies of Israel around the southern tip of the Dead Sea. As they worked their way up 'the king's highway' (Numbers 20:14–21 and Numbers 21:21–30), they encountered the people groups well established in the land. Interestingly, all three major races were relatives! First, they passed by the land of Edom (Jacob's brother Esau's descendants). The Edomites had replaced the Horims, or Horites (Deuteronomy 2:12), the giants who first lived around the mountain of Seir. Their name means 'cave-dwellers'. There are those who feel that the Horims were related to the Emims and the Rephaims which links them to the original giants. This gigantic race of aboriginal inhabitants left behind hundreds of caves in the sandstone cliffs and mountains of Edom. The most famous of the site is Petra. Was Job speaking of this giant race in Job 30:6–7? They were well-established in the region that would be known as Edom in the days of Abraham (Genesis 14:6, 36:20–21, 29)!

Edom took the place of the Horims and Lot's children took the place of the Emmims and Zuzims. The tragic beginning of the Moabites and the Ammonites is recorded in Genesis 19 following the destruction of Sodom. Lot, Abraham's nephew, became very depressed after the death of his wife and the loss of his wealth. His daughters took advantage of his daily drinking and bore two children by their father: "And the first born bare a son, and called his name Moab: the same is the father of the Moabites unto this day. And the younger, she also bare a son, and called his name Benammi: the same is the father of the children of Ammon unto this day." (Genesis 19:37–38) It was by the grace of God that despite the sin of Esau (Genesis 25:34) and the sin of Lot (II Peter 2:7–8) God still blessed these men and used their descendants to begin the destruction of Satan's Super Soldiers on the East Bank of the Jordan. Often despite our shortcomings God still can use us for His glory and the fulfillment of His divine plans (Romans 8:28).

What Moses called 'a land of giants' was already nearly purged of 'giants' by the time he arrived with the children of Abraham. God knew that there would be plenty of 'giants' (Anakims) for the children of God to fight and deal with, but God wanted them to know that whatever they would face that He had already faced and dealt with: Lucifer's large legions. If He had helped the Moabites, Ammonites, and Edomites deal with the 'giants' of their land, then He would help the Israelites deal with the 'giants' they would find in their Promised land. They were 'great' and 'many' and 'tall', but each in turn had been annihilated. The key is this phrase: **"the Lord destroyed them before them!"** The people of Israel were going to have to face the Anakims, the very 'giants' that had kept their parents out of the land (Numbers 13:33), for nearly 40 years. God had demonstrated on the east bank of the Jordan what He would do on the west bank of the Jordan. Canaan was also a land of 'giants', just like the land of Edom, Moab, and Ammon had been a land of 'giants'. God had destroyed the Rephaims, the Zuzims, and the Emmims (and perhaps other races that had been giants: the Horims and Avims (Deuteronomy 2:23), and He would help Israel destroy the Anakims as well.

I believe we have a marvellous precept here for our ongoing spiritual struggle against the 'giants' that we face. In another 'giant' story we will learn this concept: **"the battle is the Lord's"** (I Samuel 17:47). We are called to "fight the good fight" (I Timothy 6:12), but the fight is the Lord's. We are called to "war a good warfare" (I Timothy 1:18), but the war is the Lord's. Through Moses, the Lord was asking the Israelites to fight, battle, and go to war against the Anakims, but that He would destroy them before them, just like He did with their relatives in another time. We serve a Captain (Hebrews 2:10) that doesn't drive His troops, but leads His soldiers. There has not been a path you have walked that the Good Lord has no walked before you (Hebrews 4:15). It is important for us to know that God leads; He never drives (Psalm 23). When we confront our giant, God will be there before us, to prepare the battlefield for the defeat of our foe. As the simple line in a children's chorus says: "David threw the stone, and God did the rest!" When will we realize that ultimately: **"the battle is the Lord's"**, even a battle with a giant.

Israel had arrived at the borderland of the giants. They were still 'many' and "great" and "tall". What would Israel do this time? The first time they ran with fear; they refused to fight, journey on. This time however, before they confronted the Anakims they would see the ruins of three great giant races. In the place of those three gigantic groups of inhabitants of the land east of the Jordan were ordinary people, their own relatives: the Edomites, Moabites, and Ammonites, if their relatives could conquer 'giants', could they not conquer 'giants'? Remember, 'the gates of hell' (Matthew 16:18) are not able to prevail against us either. We are not to retreat from 'a land of giants', but we are to attack with boldness and courage and confidence knowing that our Commander is marching ahead of us "destroying giants"! Will we, as they did, rise up and claim and conquer 'a land of giants'?

Let me give you this last word of encouragement as you face down your giant. It was through the letter of Paul to the Romans that we were given this grand precept: **"If God be for us, who can be against us?"** (Romans 8:31) That includes 'giants' in my book. You and God make an undefeatable force even when the foe is 'many', 'great', and 'tall'. Granted, outnumbered, but never outmatched. Granted, outsized, but never overcome. Granted, outvoted, but never outdone. Sometimes we feel pretty small when we invade 'a land of 'giants', but with the Almighty by our side we have nothing to fret about or fear!

11

VICTORY OVER THE GIANT OG

Numbers 21:33-And they turned and went up by way of Bashan: and **OG THE KING OF BASHAN** went out against them, he and all his people, to the battle of Edrei.

W. GLYN EVANS HAS written in his devotional book "Daily with the King" these words: **"The life of victory begins, not with a sense of fullness, but with a sense of emptiness!"** Such was the case with the children of Israel after a forty year trek from Egypt to Eschol. During those four decades, they were a nation without a country, a people without a land, but that all changed at the Battle of Edrei. The territory of OG the giant (Deuteronomy 3:11) was the second kingdom (Sihon of Jahaz was the first-Numbers 21:21–32) conquered in the long war that would end in their conquest of Canaan. Finally, after the Battle of Jahaz and Edrei, the stigma of the failure at Kadash would begin to be forgotten, why? Because up to that point Israel had only lived in one defeat after another! After the Battles of the Red Sea (Exodus 14:15–31) and Rephidim (Exodus 17:8–16), the Israelites suffered a series of setbacks because of their refusal to enter the Promised Land God's way, but now with a new generation leading the way, the victories would come one after the other. Such is sometimes the case with the pilgrim Christian, for we too will only get to our promised land, our Beulah Land, by way of victory, not defeat. However, we must take seriously what Amy Carmichael use to say, **"We have all eternity to celebrate the victories, but**

only a few hours before sunset to win them!" To which I would only add a hearty Amen and Amen. (Psalm 72:19)

"The story is told of the great Carthaginian general, Hannibal, who summoned his troops to meet in the foothills of the towering Alps. Pointing to the majestic mountains, he said, 'Over the Alps lays Italy!' Beautiful, sunny Italy, the land of their dreams! The challenge was theirs! A challenge that meant heroism, bravery, determination! Those mountains held a lure for the brave soldiers. But, were they now ready to accept the challenge, to face the difficulties, to defeat the giant, and to hazard their lives in the undertaking to make their dreams come true? Their general did not hide from them the perils they must encounter if they were to reach the top. But he told them of the wide horizons that would be theirs at the trail's end, the honors awaiting them as a reward for their valiant act. A few retreated, preferring to live in the valley and the lowland rather than face the struggle, deadly insensitive to their glorious privilege of winning the prize! Giant obstacles had to be overcome, but the majority girded themselves for the feat to accomplish. They had caught the vision and were content to leave the valley road for high climbing. Their leader, like Moses, became famous in name and deed, and their act of heroism known, but their names remained unknown. Day by day, over sharp rocks and crags they went, through toils and pain, fainting oft from hunger and fatigue. Blood drops on the pure white snow marked their tracks. At last, cold, ragged, and hungry, they reached the top and planted their standard on the highest peak of the Alps. The almost insurmountable mountains below them were wreathed in the mystery of the clouds! The peaks around were touched with the glory of the sunrise! Before their vision, of unsurpassing loveliness, were fields of waving grain in the green valley below! Beautiful orchards, sparkling fountains! Italy! They had arrived in the land of their dreams! It lay across the Alps!" So writes Mrs. Charles Cowman in her devotional "Mountain Trailways for Youth". Even though we don't know exactly how Moses and Joshua and Caleb and the people of Israel felt in their moment of seeing the Promised Land for the first time, I can't help but think they had similar feelings as Hannibal and his men. This too was the feeling of the Israelites after their titanic struggle with the giant OG at the Battle of Edrei. The giant that blocked their view, but now they could see clearly 'the land that flowed with milk and honey'. The giant that once blocked their vision was gone, and they could see beyond. He would block their way no more!

There are times when we just can't avoid a fight. As long as we are 'strangers and pilgrims' (I Peter 2:11) in this old world, we will always be confronted and blocked by some obstacle, some giant, and if we are to continue on, press on, we must fight on. Maybe this poem by James Roberts Gilmore will comfort and encourage you when an OG blocks your progress and obscures your view: "So much to do; so little done. Ah, yester night I saw the sun, sink beamless down the vaulted gray, the ghastly ghost of yesterday. So little done; so much to do. Each morning breaks on conflicts new; but eager, brave I'll join the fray and fight the battle of today. So much to do, so little done. But when it's over, the victory won. O then my soul this strike and sorrow, will end in that great glad tomorrow!" The Israelites had gotten up on the day of the Battle of Edrei hopeful the day would bring a day of marching their army not a day of mustering their army. They were almost within sight of their destination, just one more good march and their hellish journey would be complete, over, but instead of walking they would be warring before the sun was set. The journey delayed, they stopped and fought a giant that blocked their way. At times each and every one of us will have to do the same!

Dr. C. E. Matthews once wrote, **"Seventy-five percent of victory depends on preparation!"** After nearly 40 years under the capable leadership of Joshua, Moses' general, the army of Israel was ready for this fight; this fight against the last giant of Bashan. Toughened by days of marching and drilling, the soldiers of Israel sweep aside the army of OG with ease. Walking and warfare go hand in hand in the spiritual struggle as well. The Christian soldier has his "...feet shod with the preparation of the gospel of peace..." (Ephesians 6:15) So often when we preachers zero in on this classic verse by the pen of Paul we only see the word 'gospel', for most of us are Gospel preachers. I believe we often fail to highlight and underline the word *'preparation'*! I believe one of the reasons we so often lose in the spiritual battles we fight is our lack of preparation. We will win through Christ, we are guaranteed victory in Christ, but we must be prepared for victory. Some believers just don't know how to win! Paul also wrote, "If a man therefore purge himself from these, he will be a vessel unto honor sanctified and meet for the Master's use, and PREPARED unto every good work." (II Timothy 2:21) And those good works included warring a good warfare (I Timothy 1:18). Paul also taught us that through the Word of God (II Timothy 3:16) we believers (soldiers) "the man of God" can be "...throughly furnished unto all good works." (II Timothy 3:17) Furnished

43

and prepared to take on giants like OG and win; come off the field of battle victorious. I believe Israel didn't want to fight, but she was ready to fight! And so must we!

Moses' victory over OG was complete: "So they smote him, and his sons, and all his people, until there was none left him alive: and they possessed his land." (Numbers 21:35) I believe we too will ultimately defeat our enemies. We too have been promised victory (I Corinthians 15:57 and II Corinthians 2:14) in our fight against giants. Ours might not be giant men, but gigantic sins and there is always the giant of self that haunts us and hounds us every step of the way, but furnished with the Word of God and prepared by the Spirit of God we too will come off the battlefield of Edrei victorious!

12

A LESSON IN KILLING A GIANT

Deuteronomy 1:4-After he had **SLAIN** Sihon the king of the Amorites, which dwelt in Heshbon, and **OG THE KING OF BASHAN**, which dwelt at Astaroth in Edrei.

I JUST NOTICED THIS; after Moses killed a giant he wrote a book! (Deuteronomy 1:5)

Years later when Rahab of Jericho told the spies why the Canaanites feared the Jews: it was the news of the death of OG and other events that convinced them that the Israelites were a mighty people: "For we have heard how the Lord dried up the water of the Red Sea for you, when ye came out of Egypt; and what ye did unto the two kings of the Amorites, that were on the other side of the Jordan, Sihon and OG, whom ye utterly destroyed. And as soon as we had heard these things, our hearts did melt, neither did there remain any more courage in any man, because of you: for the Lord your God, He is God in heaven above, and in earth beneath." (Joshua 2:10–11) They must have reasoned that any people that could kill OG and his nation could destroy them. A simple reading of the Bible reveals that King OG had a fearful reputation, and perhaps, was considered the mightiest man in the region? For an interesting observation on the death of OG, let me quote the famous Hebrew historian Josephus: "When matters were come to this state, OG, the king of Gilead (remember, Bashan and Gilead are the same regions in northeast Canaan) and Gaulanitis, fell upon the Israelites. He brought his army with him, and he came in haste to the assistance of his friend Sihon; but though he found him already slain, yet did he resolve still to come and fight the Hebrews, supposing he should be too hard for them, and being desirous to try their valour; but failing of his hope, he was both himself slain in the battle, and all his army was destroyed. So Moses passed over the river Jabbok, and overran the kingdom of OG. He overthrew their cities, and slew all their inhabitants, who yet exceeded in riches all the men in that part of the continent, on account of the goodness of the soil (still one of the richest land areas in Israel today), and the great quantity in their wealth. Now OG had very few equals, either in the largeness of his body or handsomeness of his appearance. He was also a man of great activity in the use of his hands, so that his actions were not unequal to the vast largeness and handsome appearance of his body; and men could easily guess at his strength and magnitude when they took his bed at Rabbath, the royal city of the Ammonites; its structure was of iron, its breadth four cubits (six feet), and its length a cubit more than double (13 ½ feet) thereto. However, his fall did not only improve the circumstance of the Hebrews for the present, but by his death he was the occasion of further good success to them; for they presently took those sixty cities which were encompassed with excellent walls, and had been subject to him; and all got both in general and in particular a great prey."

OG was no doubt proud from his defeat of all his surrounding enemies (like Adonibezek-Judges 1:4–7), and he thought this rag tag army of wandering Jews would be an easy prey, but he ran straight into a well-prepared and wonderfully trained army of determined soldiers that weren't going to let a giant and his army block their passage to the Promised Land. There was no doubt about the outcome the minute the battle was engaged, and there is no doubt about the outcome of our battles if we enter them well-equipped and well-prepared by our general the Lord Jesus Christ. The Christian should expect success, victory. Paul has told us, "Now thanks be unto God, which ALWAYS causeth us to triumph in Christ." (II Corinthians 2:14) Victory is our right by Christ, if we are ready for it; even over 'giants'. The problem today is most Christians are just winging it. Instead of taking the time to prepare for a spiritual encounter, they waste away their days of preparation, so on the day of battle they go into the fray either with their sword (the Word of God) sheathed (on the shelf) or dull (unlearned)! The Bible says there is only one way to prepare for spiritual battle: "Study to shew thyself approved unto God, a workman (warrior) that needeth not to be ashamed, rightly dividing (wheeling) the word of truth." (II Timothy

2:15) And if you do, the Bible tells us that the man of God will be prepared for all good words (II Timothy 3:16–17), including the killing of a giant!

In the dividing of OG's lands among the tribes, this section fell into the hands of the tribe of Reuben and the tribe of Gad. (Joshua 13:17–26) Yet herein lays a danger in possessing the territory of a giant. Reuben and Gad leave us with a haunting warning. **Never should we allow a victory over a giant to become a fatal weakness!** Remember, that sin's prime targets are not victims (sin already has them), but victors. Paul tells us in the spiritual struggle that, "…and having done all, to stand." (Ephesians 6:13) Even after the victory we must still be on the alert, even when the giant is dead at our feet. In just a few short weeks, Balaam would corrupt the victors of Edrei in this newly conquered land (Numbers 22–25-the next event described after the killing of OG-Numbers 21:31–35). Victory is sweet, but fleeting; gratifying but dangerous. The battle against OG was over, but it was only one victory in the eternal struggle that was the Promised Land, and we all know that one battle doesn't win the war! So it is with us as well as us wage war on sin, self, and Satan himself. We must quickly realize that there will be another battle and another battle and we must be ready for them; by keeping our celebration short. Without fail another foe will face us tomorrow in our ongoing pilgrimage through this giant infested world. Let us not get too comfortable in our gigantic victory, in our new found success against the 'giants' that we forget to keep our sentries posted, our guards alert! John Yates wrote in his third stanza of "Faith is the Victory" these compelling words, "On every hand the foe we find, drawn up in dread array. Let tents of ease be left behind and onward to the fry." Too many Christians are settling in, instead of pushing on; getting comfortable instead of preparing for another battle; planning a victory party, instead of sharping their sword for another fight. It is not time yet to stop and gather our spoils, take a rest, and build monuments to our victory over a giant. Moses didn't spend much time pondering his victory over OG or writing about his killing OG; he left that to other historians (Joshua 2:10, I Kings 4:19, Nehemiah 9:22, Psalm 135:11, and Josephus) and so should we, there will be time for celebration when we get to heaven!

The greatest lesson we can learn about killing a giant is the fact that wasn't our last giant to kill. W. Glyn Evans writes this in a favorite devotional "Daily with the King": "Every disciple of Jesus Christ must come to terms with the problem of **continuance**. As a disciple I have known moments of ecstasy and glory (like killing a giant), but also moments of sorry, failure, and defeat (for being unprepared for the next fight). How do I continue victoriously instead of enjoying victory only now and then? In the words of J. Taylor Smith, how do I '*__abide and abound__*'? In a sense, I must not be occupied with victory, for victory is a result of a previously met pair of conditions." Evans was reminding us that the Battle of Edrei is over and the giant OG is killed, but that won't guarantee tomorrows victory if we are not prepared. Giants fall, giants are killed, giants are defeated, but we must fight on! Victory can sometimes be our biggest stumbling block and Satan knows it. What OG couldn't do Balaam almost did (Revelation 2:14)!

13

BATTLEGROUND
THE GIANT'S LAND

Deuteronomy 3:13-And the rest of Gilead, and all Bashan, being the kingdom of OG, gave I unto the half-tribe of Manasseh; all the region of Argob, with all Bashan, which is called **THE LAND OF THE GIANTS.**

LET US LOOK ONCE more at the land of OG, for I would like for you to consider this concept I learned from the famous pastor, and for me, a great devotional writer, A. W. Tozer. In an article entitled, *"This World: Playground or Battleground?"* Tozer writes:

> "In the early days, when Christianity exercised a dominant influence over the American thinking, men were convinced the world was a battleground. Our fathers believed in sin and the Devil and hell as constituting one force; and they believed in God and righteousness and heaven as the other. There were in the nature of them forever opposed to each other in deep, grave, irreconcilable hostility. Man, so our fathers held, had to choose sides; he could not be neutral. The fight would be real and deadly and would last as long as life continued here below. Man looked forward to heaven as a man returning from the wars, a laying down of the sword to enjoy in peace the home prepared for them. The Christian soldier thought of home and rest and reunion, and his voice grew plaintive as he sung of battles ended and victory won. But whether he was charging into enemy guns,

**or dreaming of war's end and the father's 'welcome home', he
never forgot what kind of world he lived in. It was a battleground, and many were the wounded and the slain."**

All the aspects of these thoughts can be testified too in the battle for
OG's land, the last battle for the land on the east bank of the Jordan River.
If the children of Israel forgot anything in their battle for Canaan, it was
the revelation that Tozer reveals in his devotional. Ultimately, the battle is
never over, the war will go on generation to generation, and let us never
forget, *'the last mile of the way'* will take us through a battlefield, not a
playground! So many Christians today are playing in Florida when they
ought to be battling the Devil in Maine. The playground of the 'rich and
famous' continue some believers who have stopped fighting and are playing out their final mile in pleasure rather than in helping the Church war a
good warfare against sin and Satan. What is this lesson from 'the land of the
giants' that we need to learn again?

When Balaam failed in his attempt to curse the children of Israel
(Numbers 22–24), he did not give up, or in. **When he found he could not
turn the Lord against Israel, he found he could turn Israel against the
Lord.** "Behold, these caused the children of Israel, though the counsel of
Balaam, to commit trespass against the Lord in the matter of Peor." (Numbers 31:16) It was Balaam that introduced Israel to Canaanite fornication
and Canaanite idolatry. The battleground of the East bank (the land of the
giants) had turned into a playground. "And Israel abode in Shittin, and the
people began to commit whoredom with the daughters of Moab. And they
called the people unto the sacrifices of their gods, and the people did eat,
and bowed down to their gods." (Numbers 25:1–2) Has this not happened
today in the Church of Christ? Christians no longer think of the world as
a battlefield, but a place to have fun, to party, to enjoy themselves. "We are
not here to fight, but to have fun," some say. We are not here to fight but to
frolic! Sexual sins in the Church are as commonplace as in the red-light dis-
trict of any inter-city. We have Balaam's ministers standing up every Sunday
saying, "It is lawful for you to have her, or him, and it is lawful for him to
have him and her to have her!" John the Baptist never forgot that he was
in a battle and to dine with the Herod's might save his life, and not to stop
fighting would cost him his head! Satan has tricked us like Balaam tricked
Israel into thinking, we have arrived, we have won, the battle is over, the
victory has been won, and now it is time to play, to party!

The war against OG was designed by God to show Israel how they must always fight against OG's philosophy, OG's idolatrous apostasy, and that killing a giant in his own land isn't enough. We often forget to understand the depth of these lines in the Book of Judges: "Now these are the nations which the Lord left, to prove Israel by them, even as many of Israel as had not known all the wars of Canaan; only that the generation of the children of Israel might know, **to teach them war....**" (Judges 3:1-2) God knows if you are to survive on this planet you need to know war, not whoredom. What was true for Israel in Canaan is true for the Church today. James writes: "Ye adulterers, and adulteresses, know ye not that the friendship of the world is enmity with God? Whosoever therefore will be a friend of the world is the enemy of God." (James 4:4) Israel had been convinced by Balaam in the land of the giants that they could co-exist, co-habit with the philosophy and the gods of the giant, if not the giant himself. Satan is willing every time to sacrifice a giant for a compact of friendship. An alliance over fighting is preferred even by the Devil Himself, especially when he knows that the fine print in the agreement means a mutual understanding, cooperation, and compromise were the catch words then as now resulting in playing not fighting. Balaam's lie was" Isn't it more fun, more profitable to play with each other than to prey on each other?" Israel failed to see that in the end, that they were the prey, and so are we (I Peter 5:8)!

The Church and the average Christian has swallowed the same hook! Cooperation and compromise, instead of conflict and conquest have become the philosophy of the Church in the early years of the twenty-first century. We have beaten our swords into plow shears too soon (Isaiah 2:4). We have given up our war horse for a rocking horse, or rocking chair too soon. We have given up our frontline positions for a sunny spot in Florida. Our vocation has become our vacation! **We have made peace with the world, but don't realize that the world has not made peace with us.** We have signed a non-aggression pact with Islam, not realizing that Islam is still on the attack. So while the Church parties on and has Sunday picnics, the world, the wicked, and the Wicked One are marching unopposed across the face of the earth. We think we are safe in our peaceful enclaves, but the day will come when our enemy will be at the door and only a rescue mission (called the rapture) from heaven will save us, why? Because we have forgotten that this world is a battleground not a playground! Our mission is to fight our last battle and die, sword in hand, shield raised high. We have too many old soldiers dying on the sands of Florida instead of the sands of

Iwo Jima (a famous World War Two battlefield). We are losing too many warriors in the lights of a playground than the lines of a battleground!

I like what Martin Luther once said in a sermon: "The Devil held a great anniversary at which his emissaries were convened to report the results of their several missions. 'I let loose the wild beasts of the desert,' said one, 'on a caravan of Christians and their bones are now bleaching on the sands.' 'What of that?' said the Devil? 'Their souls were all saved.' 'I drove the east wind,' said another, 'against a ship freighted with Christians, and they were all drowned.' What of that?' said the Devil, 'Their souls were all saved?

'For ten years I tried to get a single Christian asleep,' said a third, 'and I succeeded and left him so!' Then the Devil shouted, 'and the night stars of hell sang for joy.' One of the tricks of Satan is to make us believe that submission to God means a spiritual stupor. Far from it. It is a battle, it is resistance and first of all to Satan himself." Amen and Amen!

14

THE MAKING OF A GIANT-KILLER

Joshua 13:12-All the kingdom of Og in Bashan, which reigned in Ashtaroth
and in Edrei, who remained of the remnant of the giants, **FOR THESE DID
MOSES SMITE**, and cast them out.

EVEN YEARS AFTER MOSES slew the last east bank giant, Joshua was recording that exploit as he recorded his victorious triumphs in Canaan (Joshua
12–13). On my first trip to India in 2006, I had the privilege to preach
fourteen times at Kerala Baptist Bible College chapels. In 2007, I only got
one chance but my theme was 'the making of a giant-killer'. This devotional
in our Satan's Super Soldiers series will center around the outline I used in
that challenge and the personal characteristics it takes to take on a giant
and win. My daughter Marnie was with me in 2007 and after her testimony
and our singing Philip Bliss' hymn "Dare To Be A Daniel", I share my interpretation on the Biblical qualities it takes to face down and defeat one
of Satan's mightiest 'giants': OG! Moses is given the credit for killing this
super-soldier, despite, the fact that he was nearly 120 at the time (Deuteronomy 34:7). As was the case in those days, often the commander was
given credit for the victory even though another soldier probably delivered
the fatal blow. I don't actually believe that Moses was in battle at his advance
years, so my belief it was either Joshua (Exodus 17:9) or Caleb (Joshua
14:14–15), but whoever brought OG down, he had these virtues, virtues we
will see in all the giant-killers highlighted in this book!

In Bliss' song mentioned above, he wrote this line: "Many giants, great and tall, stalking through the land, headlong to the earth would fall, if met by Daniel's Band?" I have wondered his choice of Daniel over David because the Bible never record's Daniel and his band (Hananiah, Mishael, and Azariah-Daniel 1:6) facing any giants unless it was the giant statue of Nebuchadnezzar (Daniel 3:1–90 feet tall) or the large lions Daniel faced (Daniel 6:21)? He could have written about Moses' Band (Joshua and Caleb) or David's Band of giant-killers (II Samuel 21:15–22). Perhaps, that is what Bliss was getting at; it takes a band, a group to kill a giant, or maybe, like John Bunyan, he was using an analogy of 'the giant'. Bunyan's Giant Despair is a classic, but in the case of Moses and OG this is the story of an ordinary man facing an extra-ordinary man and coming out the victor instead of a victim. So what makes such a man a 'giant-killer'? Consider these five characteristics I share with the students at KBBC:

1. **BE OBEDIENT.** When God tells you to take on a giant, you need to do it. God told Moses to deal with the giants of the Promised Land and Moses did. Moses was use to obeying God; whether a giant or not (Ephesians 6:1). Giant-killers are made not born. Our basic instinct is to disobey just like our first parents, but a child of God that is taught to obey will eventually not question the command; even if that command is to take on a giant! Moses was near the end of his life when he slew OG. Moses wasn't always obedient (Numbers 20:1–13) and his act of disobedience with striking the rock instead of speaking to the rock would keep him out of the Promised Land, but when it came to fighting OG he obeyed. If God tells us to attack a giant, it is God's job, as we have learned, to fight for us, but our job is to obey. **"Obedience is the very best way to show that you believe; doing exactly what the Lord commands, doing it happily!"** (children's chorus) Obedience is the first essential ability of a 'giant-killer'!

2. **BE RESPONSIBLE.** Some people have the popular misconception that a new command from God releases them from their current responsibilities. Not so! If we show responsibility in one area, God will give us responsibilities in other areas. This is the teaching of the parable of the talents! (Matthew 25:14–30) Moses had been found a responsible leader, as had Joshua and Caleb. They were the only three left of the entire older generation of Israelites that had come out of Egypt. Even Aaron and Miriam had died by this time. The reason they

were invading the land of giants was because they had been found responsible stewards of God's people. They had turned the nation around. They had trained a complete new generation to trust and obey God; no matter His commands. When the giant OG died, his death was just one act in a long list of responsible deeds.

3. **BE FAITHFUL.** Moses had been faithful in delivering the children of Israel from bondage in Egypt. He had been found faithful leading the people to Mount Sinai to receive the Ten Commandments. Despite the disobedience of the first generation of people at Kadash, Moses, Joshua, and Caleb had been found faithful (Hebrews 11:6) to God's Word. They pleaded and bagged the people to follow them into the Promised Land, a land of giants, but they refused (I Corinthians 4:2). Faithfulness is a key ingredient in a 'giant-killer' whether in private, as Moses experienced in the hills of Midian, or in public, as Moses proved in the battle against OG (Luke 19:17). Your neighbor's unfaithfulness or your family's unfaithfulness doesn't have to rub off on you.

4. **BE YOURSELF.** We will discover as we study our way through the 'giants' in Satan's army that each giant-killer was his own man. (Matthew 6:27) Whether giants in Basham or giants in Gath, the foe might change but we can't! David would fight his first giant with a sling and a stone (I Samuel 17) and his last giant with a sword and shield (II Samuel 21). I am convinced that many Christians have given up using the Bible as they know it; to quote a modern philosopher: **"Use what works and stay with it!"** Use what you know and stay with it. A child who only knows a few verses of Scriptures can fight just as affectively as the Bible student of many years. Be yourself means to be you, don't try to fight another man's way because God can use you your way and your brother in Christ his way. If I have learned anything in my study of the giants, it is God uses the giant-killer as he is and with what he has to use! (What is in your hand?-Exodus 4:2)

5. **BE A BELIEVER.** The last and most important characteristic in a giant-killer is the ability to believe that he can win against any giant, including the giant Satan! All of Saul's army saw Goliath as too big to fight (I Samuel 17:11), while David saw Goliath as to big to miss! **Courage comes with confidence.** Remember how often in this study we have talked about how Moses had put his confidence in the Lord. The reason the first generation Israeli failed to confront the giants is

their lack of trust in God's help. They ran from the giants because they lacked the bravery and belief they could win with God. As we face the spiritual giants of our day (Ephesians 6:12), we too must believe we can win (I Corinthians 15:57).

Are you ready to be a 'giant-killer'? We will see more qualifications as we continue our study of Satan's super soldiers, but we have the five pillars needed for the foundation, the ground on which we must stand when we confront our giant. Start working on these characteristics now, so that on the day you are called to the battlefield you will be ready!

15

REMEMBERING THE GIANT OG

Psalm 136:20-And **OG THE KING OF BASHAN**; for His mercy endureth forever.

BEFORE WE LEAVE THE east bank of the Jordan 'giants' and trace the Anakims, I would like for you to notice that of all the Rephaims: OG is mentioned 22 times and in 6 different books of the Bible. Why did God want the Israelites to remember OG? Why would God recall to our attention this particular giant so many times? From the books of Moses to the psalms of David, OG is mentioned again and again. I believe there is another lesson that God would have us learn from the life and death of the giant OG!

In my study of this mighty king of Bashan, I have come to the conclusion that OG was a product of intermarriage of the Rephaims and the Amorites. This deduction comes from the fact that OG was both a king of the Amorites, and the last of the Rephaims (Deuteronomy 3:11). His 60 city kingdom was located in the Argod, a 60 by 20 mile territory rising nearly thirty feet above the Bashan plain. This rocky bastion would have been nearly impregnable to the Israelites if OG would have chosen to remain there. But as we have learned, OG instead chose to come out of his fortress plateau and face the Jews at Edrei (Numbers 21:33–35). Would OG have ultimately been safe in the natural defenses of the Argod (Deuteronomy 3:4)? Would OG have been safe anywhere?

I believe OG, like the other obstacles Satan put in the way of the Israelites, was destined to fall! I believe God saw the necessity of Israel facing such a foe and coming forth victorious. One of the important lessons in battle is to remember your victories. I have noticed must of my spiritual life that _the Devil wants me to remember my defeats and forget my victories._ He wants me to remember the prayers that haven't been answered yet, and forget the ones that have. He encourages me to remember my weaknesses and to forget my strengths; my disappointments not my successes. God is just the opposite. In the Word of God the lesson of OG was one of defeat, destruction, death to a giant; having been overpowered, conquered by God. There is a very interesting verse in Joshua's last speech to Israel that helps us understand this precept: "And I sent the hornet before you, which drave them out from before you, even the two kings of the Amorites (Sihon and OG); but not with thy sword, not with thy bow." (Joshua 24:12) Was OG defeated by tiny hornets? Wouldn't that have been poetic justice?

Joshua was recalling the battle for the land on the east bank of the Jordan. We have already speculated that Sihon might have been a giant like OG, but we have no proof other than their connection. But this we do know from our research into these east bank battles, that these 'two kings of the Amorites' are mentioned together and often. I have already mentioned how often OG is mentioned in Scriptures; Sihon is mentioned 37 times and in eight books of the Bible; almost half again as many as OG! According to Joshua, and he was there at both battles, they were driven out and defeated by 'hornets'? A. R. Fausset makes this amazing observation about these unique battles: "God therefore saw it needful to encourage Israel in facing a foe (OG), 'fear him not'; and God sent hornets which, as well as infatuation, drove OG into the open field where he was overthrown!" Evidence is little, a verse here and a verse there, but could that be the reason that OG left his mighty fortresses for the open ground of Edrei: hornets? But what is very clear to me is the truth that God never wanted Israel to forget the amazing victory He and they won over these 'two kings of the Amorites' and especially over the giant OG. Have we forgotten Satan has already been defeated?

Another reason I believe in the importance of remembering and re-calling the fall of the giant OG is the reference to his burial plot. As we have seen in other chapters, the sarcophagus of this giant was a tourist destina-tion, a tourist attraction famous in it day. We figured by the standard of the cubit that OG's single bed was 13 ½ feet long and 6 feet wide (Deu-teronomy 3:11) and that he was probably bigger and taller than Goliath: only a nine footer? OG could have been 11 or 12 feet tall by any stretch of the imagination. Years later the prophet Amos spoke of the Amorites with this description; "....height like that of the cedars and strong as the oaks." (Amos 2:9) By the time Moses wrote of OG's bedstead, this gigantic relic was at Rabbath of Ammon. Some scholars believe this happened this way. After the battle the Ammonites followed the Israelites and as pillagers took possession of this powerful symbol of the great giant and put the artifact on display! Or could have the Israelites sent the trophy of war to their cousins (remember the Ammonites were the descendants of Lot's (Abraham's nephew) son Ammon) as a symbol of God's order not to attack their relatives the Ammonites? Perhaps, to show them that their God was more powerful than the 'giants'? Whatever the reason, the lesson is being rehearsed again and again that Jehovah is greater than a giant.

A Doctor Geddes conjectures that OG didn't die at the Battle of Edrei, but escaped the fight and sought sanctuary among the Ammonites where he eventually died from wounds he received at the battle. That the iron bedstead was actually OG's coffin made out of black basalt. It seems that the Arab's in that region call basalt 'iron' because it does contain 20% of the metal. OG's bier could have been a huge black basalt sarcophagus, and the place of his burial, or death became a place of interest for those who passed by because of its size. So whatever version or interpretation of OG's death and burial you believe, the important truth for me is that through the hands of Moses the end of this giant happened: directly or indirectly and God wanted the Jews to remember it down through the ages as an example of what they could do with God on their side (Romans 8:31)!

I chose the verse printed above because it contains my final challenge to this remembrance. God's unique intervention for Israel against the giant OG became a theme of praise: "Praise the Lord; for the Lord is good....Who smote great nations, and slew mighty kings; Sihon king of the Amorites, and OG king of Bashan....and gave their land for an heritage, an heritage unto Israel His people." (Psalm 135: 3, 10–12) It was through the 'mercy' of the Lord that OG was killed. On their own, in their own strength, the defeat would have been impossible. So what is it that needs to be remembered about OG? That he was big, a mighty king, a powerful giant? No! OG is to be remembered so that we might 'praise the Lord'; that we might remember 'His mercy endureth forever'! ***It has more to do with remembering God than remembering OG!*** It is more about remembering God's mercy than OG's might. When our foes are recalled, it is for the purpose of remembering how our God defeated them. Too many find their fascination in the wrong object of remembrance. ***It is not OG, but God!*** I believe the psalm-ist described this lesson about remembering 'giants' best when he wrote: "One generation shall praise Thy works to another, and shall declare Thy mighty acts!" (Psalm 145:4) One of the mightiest acts recorded in God's Word about God is His defeat of OG, and through the writers of the Bible from generation to generation the defeat of OG is rewritten again and again (Numbers 32:33, Joshua 9:2, I Kings 4:19, Nehemiah 9:22). One of the first book projects I ever tackled was a look into "Thy Mighty Acts" (title of the book). It was my way of reminding me again of the works of God I remem-bered from my childhood!

16

ANAK
THE FEARED GIANT

Numbers 13:33-And there we saw **THE GIANTS, THE SONS OF ANAK, WHICH COME OF THE GIANTS:** and we were in our own sight as grasshoppers, and so we were in their sight.

ONE BY ONE WE are profiling Satan's important 'giants'. If Rephaim was the first (after the flood) giant, and Arba was the future (first of another distinct race of giants) giant, then Anak was the feared (fear of the sons of this giant kept the Israelites out of Canaan for forty years) giant. Long before the Jews confronted OG, they were scared away from the Promised Land by 'the sons of Anak'. "Fee...fi...fo...fum....I smell the blood of a Hebrew's son" was about all it took to set the Israelites to flight!

When it comes to warfare with Anak, one of the first enemies that must be conquered is 'fear'! Fear is the archenemy of any soldier, but let me say this from the outset of this devotional that I do not believe that to be afraid is in itself a sin. It is like a temptation; to be tempted is not a sin, but yielding to temptation is a sin (James 1:12–15). The same is true with fear; fear in and of itself is not a sin, but yielding to fear can be a sin! We all admire the man who fears sin. We all look for the doctor that fears disease. We entrust our money to the banker that fears debt, do we not? We love the child that fears the road and stays away from it, and we respect the person that fears drink and what that drink or drug can do. Nowhere in the Bible can you find the commandment: **"Thou shalt no fear!"** I have come to believe that it is a useless endeavor to try and stop people from being afraid of something or someone, for fear is a God-given, built-in, natural quality of self-preservation and protection, even against Anak!

Glyn Evan's once asked this question in his devotional Book "Daily with the King": "Do not animals protect themselves by being afraid?" Another God given instinct: 'And the fear of you and the dread of you shall be upon every beast of the earth, and upon the fowl of the air, upon all that moveth upon the earth, and upon all the fishes of the sea....' (Genesis 9:2) So fear need not be ignored or laughed at, but conquered. We must learn how to engage fear on the battlefields of life and learn how to win over it. Even Jesus was known for "His Godly Fear"! (Hebrews 5:7 ASV) The wise man Solomon even said that "The fear of the Lord is the beginning of knowledge." (Proverbs 1:7) Who hasn't been afraid? Maybe we, like Joshua just before the Second Battle of Ai, are still afraid, and need to hear this from our God: "Then the Lord said unto Joshua, Do not be afraid; do not be discouraged. Take the whole army with you, and go up and attack, Ai, his people, his city, and his land." (Joshua 8:1 NIV) Joshua was taught to defeat his fears before he defeated Ai, so by the time Joshua meet Anak's kids at Hebron he had learned to control his fear of them because he had help defeat OG. That is what we must do as we face the giants of our life that cause us to fear.

The children of Israel were not the first or the last to enter a battle afraid. "And Jehoshaphat feared!" (II Chronicles 20:3) What was the cause of Jehoshaphat's fear? A massive army made up of Moabites, Ammonites, and Edomites that had invaded Judah (II Chronicles 20:1-2, 10). At the Battle of Jervel, Jehoshaphat, like Israel, had to face his fears, but also like Israel he went into battle with these words from God: "Thus saith the Lord unto you, be not afraid, nor dismayed by reason of this great (giant) multitude: for the battle is not yours, but God." (II Chronicles 20:15) **Fear must be faced with faith in God.** Israel had lost the First Battle for Canaan (Numbers 14:43-45) when they attacked after God had told them not too. Fear is especially dangerous after you have met the enemy and he has already defeated you. Each and every time fear wins; fear gets more ferrous and more formidable. It is never easy to defeat a foe who has beaten you already, and who of us has not lost in open combat with fear a few times (the curse of Anak)!

How did Israel conquer their fear of Anak? The Psalmist expresses it best with these words: ***"When I am afraid, I will put my trust in thee."*** (Psalm 56:3 ASV) At the First Battle of Canaan Israel had taken their eyes off the Lord and looked at Anak's sons. They had trusted God in the Battle of Egypt for strategy and strength, but when they came up against the Anak they thought they could do it themselves. They went into the First Battle of Canaan and soon fled in fear, whereas in the Second battle of Canaan, they went into battle afraid, but soon fought without fear when they trusted in God. Peter learned while fighting the winds and waves on the Sea of Galilee just how important these principles are: "And when Peter was come down out of the ship, he walked on the water to go to Jesus. But when he saw the wind boisterous, he was afraid; and beginning to sink he cried saying, Lord, save me." (Matthew 14:29–30) Israel first feared, and then they learned to focus their faith on God. **Face your fears with faith in God.** Look beyond the giant, high walls, the mountain, and see Jesus, '....**and the things of earth will grow strangely dim in the light of His glory and grace."** (Words in song Turn Your Eyes Upon Jesus!)

Now just because you conquered your fear of Anak doesn't mean it won't have to be faced again, for we read, "And the Lord said unto Joshua, fear them to, for I have delivered them into thine hand..." (Joshua 10:8) These words come from the very next battle in the conquest of Canaan. I have come to the conclusion in my study of fear in the Bible that though fear can be defeated I wonder if it can ever be completely conquered in one's lifetime. Each test, each battle brings its own form of fear. Remember how Peter was defeated by fear in the courtyard of Caiaphas just before Jesus' death (Matthew 26:69–75). One might think he had conquered his fear on the surface of the Sea of Galilee? Not so! Yet after the resurrection and ascension of Christ, Peter goes on to preach seemingly without fear, so we might ask has Peter finally conquered his fear? Some might say yes, but I read this in Paul's book to the Galatians: "But when Peter was come to Antioch I withstood him to the face, because he was to be blamed. For before that certain came from James, he did eat with the Gentiles: but when they were come, he withdrew and separated himself, FEARING them which were of the circumcision." (Galatians 2:11–12) No, the battle against fear is an ongoing and constant struggle in this present world. Paul wrote Timothy: "For God hath not given us the spirit of fear...." (II Timothy 1:7) Fear comes from our adversary the Devil (Hebrews 2:14–15). If we will put our complete trust and confidence in God and God alone we too in time will arrive at the battlefield against our Anak only to find that our natural fear has been eliminated by God and replaced by courage.

What I find most fascinating about the fear the sons of Anak wrought on the Israelites is the ultimate fact that eventually the giants of Canaan were defeated one by one by one, and not one giant victory is recorded. What did one of our president's once say: **"The only thing to fear is fear itself?"** Fear is a simple emotion. There is no substance to fear. It is a thought, yes, even an imagination. We fear the boggy man under the bed, but no boggy man exists. Where there giants in Canaan? Certainly! Did they have to be confronted? Certainly! I have discovered that the only real weapon the giants really possessed was the weapon of fear, and God has promised us-Isaiah 54:17. Read it!!!!!

17

THE WEST BANK ANAKIMS

Deuteronomy 1:28-Whether shall we go up? Our brothers have discouraged our hearts, saying, the people is greater and taller than we; the cities are great and walled up to heaven; and moreover we have seen **THE SONS OF THE ANAKIMS** there.

WITH THE EAST BANK of the Jordan conquered, it was now time for the Israelites to cross the Jordan River and lay claim to 'the Promised Land'! In Moses description to the second generation Jew concerning the complaints that prevented their parents from immediately moving into 'the Promised Land' from the south, he described the Anakims (Numbers 13:33). Of all the hostile people in this very hostile land, the Anakims were the most feared. We have already looked at the basic history of the Anakims starting with the giant Arba. Now it is time to understand what made these 'giants' so frightening to the Jews? It was more than their 'greatness', their 'height', their 'great cities', and their 'high walls', the very name Anak was enough to set the first generation of Jews to flight. How would Moses prepare the second generation not to run? This is what Moses told them: "Hear, O Israel: thou art to pass over Jordan this day, to go to possess nations greater and mightier than thyself, cities great and fenced up to heaven, a people great and tall, the children of the Anakims, whom thou knowest, and of whom thou has heard say, who can stand before the children of Anak?" (Deuteronomy 9:1-2) Moses wasn't mincing any words; he wasn't trying to sugar-coat the situation; he was being honest with his analysis. I believe Moses was giving the Israelites a lesson in facing your fear head on!

The Anakims were, first, **'greater'** than the Israelites in many ways. For me, Moses was telling this new group of Jews of the well-known reputation of the west bank Anakims. They had made a name for themselves over the years and their famous had spread far and wide. They had become 'great' in their own eyes, and 'great' in the eyes of others. Remember how the spies put it after they sighted them: "We were in our own eyes as grasshoppers, and so we were in their sight." (Numbers 13:33) It is part of human nature to see oneself through one's own eyes. Because of their size and successes, the Anakims saw themselves as 'greater', 'superior', 'mightier' than others. They were better in their own eyes than others, especially the small stature Israelites. In time with their reputation growing others saw them in the same light: great! What 'giants' forget is that greatness is not seen in the same light with God. "Now I know that the Lord is greater than all gods: for in the thing wherein they dwelt proudly He was above them." (Exodus 18:11) Ultimately, it is God who determines who is great and who is greater and who is greatest! This classic concept printed in James has been true since the earliest days of this planet, including the days of the 'giants': **"God resisteth the proud!"** (James 4:6) The Anakims had become proud and arrogant, and saw themselves as the 'greatest' in the land. That boxer of the 60s who called himself 'the greatest', do you know of his condition today? This is how God said He would deal with these 'greater' people: "To drive out nations from before thee greater and mightier than thou art, to bring thee in, and to give thee their land for an inheritance, as it is this day." (Deuteronomy 4:38) This included the people group known as the Anakims!

The Anakims were, second, **'taller'** than the Israelites. We still live in an age were height is significant. When one is able to look down on someone, he often feels superior, stronger, with a strategic advantage. I remember the first time I took on a taller basketball player. I was intimidated by his height; that is until my coach taught me ways around his tallness. The sheer size of these Anakims was beyond imagination to the Israelites. The only way you can really understand what they saw is to picture yourself as a child going up against an adult. I recall to this day one of my rare coaching experiences when I decided to coach my son's first basketball team. He was only in the second grade at the time, and there were very few teams of that age in the area to play. Our last game of the year was against a team of six and seventh grades. We eventually lost 71 to 4, and height did make a difference. My son's opponents could keep shooting until they scored because they stood in some cases two feet above my son. I promised my son after that game that he would never lose a basketball game like that again, and he didn't. But over time my son learned how to win and score not matter how tall his opponent was eventually ending his high school career scoring 1198 points. Such was the case with the Israelites. They were ordinary men going up against super-men, but they too learned Romans 8:31.

The Anakims were, third, **'mightier'** than the Israelites. If 'greatness' speaks of reputation and 'taller' speaks of height, then 'mightier' speaks of strength; their pure physical size would have naturally meant than they were stronger than the average Jew. I too have meet men bigger, taller, and stronger than I was. They could work longer, lift heavier loads, and through greater strength accomplish tasks I could not even imagine doing! So it was with the Anakims. They were not only powerful in combat, but they were able to build mighty fortified cities in difficult places like on top of Mount Hebron! Note carefully in the verses that I have printed in this article the phrase: **'walled up to heaven'**! The Jew wouldn't have seen such cities in Egypt. When the spies explored Canaan for the first time they were not only confronted with tall people, but tall walled cities: "Nevertheless the people be strong that dwell in the land, and the cities are walled, and very great...." (Numbers 13:28) They were not only impressed with the people but the places as well. The great people groups were famous in the ancient world for their cities. The city of Babylon was a witness to the greatness of the Chaldeans. The city of Nineveh was a testimony to the might of the Assyrians. The city of Hebron (more later) was an example of the power of the Anakims. Yet we should never forget: "For ye see your calling, breth-ren, how that...not many mighty...are called: but God hath chosen...the weak things of the world to confound the things which are mighty...that no flesh should glory in His presence." (I Corinthians 1:26–27, 29) Amen and Amen!

The west bank Anakims were a formable foe. The west bank 'giants' were an obstacle to the Jew's invasion, and these 'giants would be the great-est opponents the Israelites would face in their conquest of Canaan. They would continue to hound and haunt and harass the Hebrews for the next five hundred years or more, but despite their greatness, height, and might they would be no match for God's people throughout those years. As the Jews readied themselves for the Jordan crossing and the 'giants' beyond they claimed a promise from their leader who had died shortly before their crossing: "Then will the Lord drive out all these nations from before you, and ye shall possess greater nations and mightier than yourself." (Deuteronomy 11:23) I am convinced that the last 'mightier' was a reference to the Anakims. They too would fall before the onslaught of the Jews. History would verify that what God promised Moses and what Moses passed on to the second generation of Jews would happen. We too have been given a promise: "For the weapons of our warfare are not carnal, but mighty through God to the pulling down of stronghold." (II Corinthians 10:4) Like the Jews, claim God's promises and conquer your Anakims!

18

THE STRONGHOLD
OF THE ANAKIMS

Joshua 11:21-And at that time came Joshua, **AND CUT OFF THE ANA-
KIMS FROM THE MOUNTAINS, FROM HEBRON, FROM
DEBIR, FROM ANAB,** and from all the mountains of Judah, and from the
mountains of Israel: Joshua destroyed them utterly with their cities.

WE HAVE BEEN LOOKING into the history of the Anakims and their confrontation with the Israelites at the time of Joshua and Caleb and we found that
the roots of this giant clan can be traced back to Arba (Joshua 14:15), the
father of the Anakims; though, we feel we have been exposing them back as
far as Satan himself (Genesis 6:4)! We have also looked into **the reputation**
of the Anakims and have discovered that they were the most feared of all
the giants (Numbers 13:33) in the Bible. In this article I would like to take
you into **the refuge** of the Anakims; where this fearsome family lived. It
must have been a frightening prospect to face the last of the Rephaims on
the plateau of Bashan (Deuteronomy 3:11), but to face a gigantic race at
the height of their power and numbers in the mountains of Canaan was
another matter altogether!

The descendants of Arba settled into the mountainous country of
Southern Canaan; Satan's blocking tactic as the Israelites moved up into
Canaan from the south after leaving Egypt, and it worked for 40 years!
In their mountain refuge, the Anakims built strong towns with tall walls

surrounding them. By the time Joshua and the Israelites arrived with their armies, invading from the east this time; the giants were well entrenched with well-prepared strongholds. If we think defeating a giant in the open is tough (like David); defeating a giant behind a high battlement would seem impossible! Yet this is exactly what men like Joshua (see the verse printed above) and Caleb did. Despite the seemingly impregnable fortress on top of Mount Hebron, Caleb would ask his good friend and life-long companion: "Now therefore give me this mountain…." (Joshua 14:12). Caleb was asking for a hilltop city full of giants; whose inhabitants were the Anakims (Joshua 14: 15).

There are many kinds of strongholds. I remember in the early 60s attending classes at school against the day of an atomic attack. I still remember my Dad not being interested when I returned from school all excited about the possibility of building a bomb shelter. Dad told me that the technology for building atomic bomb would always out distance the technology for building atomic bomb shelters and that we needed to put our trust in God and if "the bomb" was dropped, heaven would be our refuge! All man-made strongholds are really inadequate when it comes to facing God, even gigantic, giant shelters. In Caleb's day a stronghold was simply a fortified city or town with a high wall made of earth or stone with a thick, heavy wooden or brass gate. Higher towers on top of the walls helped the defenders see far in advance the approach of an enemy and when your city was already on a mountaintop surprise was out of the question! Caleb had faith that with God on his side, he would be able to figure out a way to overcome the walls and defeat the giants inside. I know I have quoted this verse before, but we need to be remained again and again of the promise of God given to us through the pen of Paul: "(For the weapons of our warfare are not carnal, but mighty through God to the pulling down of strong holds.)" (II Corinthians 10:4) **Impressive though they might be, yet they are not impossible, if God is on your side.**

There are three basic standards by which all strongholds must be judged. First, any stronghold must be adequate in power to protect its citizens in any kind of attack. **Only Jesus is all-powerful.** Christ told his disciples: "All power is given me in heaven and in earth." (Matthew 28:18) How often Jesus demonstrated to His followers that He had the power to protect them; whether in the midst of a storm, in the midst of lepers, or in the midst of demon-possessed men. Jesus protected them from diseases, devils, and dangers. This reminds me of what the Psalmist once wrote: "He shall cover thee with His feathers, and under His wings shalt thou trust: His truth shall be thy shield and buckler. Thou shalt not be afraid for the terror by night; nor for the arrows that flieth by day; nor the pestilence that walketh in darkness; nor for the destruction that wasteth at noonday." (Psalm 91:4–6) A stronghold filled with Anakims has nothing on the one who has Jesus on his side. Caleb taught us this lesson at Hebron.

Second, any stronghold must be accessible and available to all who would need its security. **Only Jesus is all-providing.** He said: "He that cometh to me I will in no wise cast out." (John 6:37) The old Church hymn, "Whosoever Will" perhaps says it best: "Whosoever hearth shout, shout the sound! Spread the blessed tidings all the world around. Tell the joyful news wherever man is found. Whosoever will may come." (Romans 10:13) The stronghold of Hebron and Debir and Anab were for 'giants' only, but when Caleb finally capture these cities their gates were opened to all. Did you know this city of giants would become one of the six refuge cities? (Joshua 20:1–7) Like with cities, so with soldiers; just how many of Satan's giants have switched sides? I am thinking of men like Saul (Acts 9:1–6) who become Paul, of Augustine! Remember, Jerusalem might not have been a city of giants, but it was once the city of the wicked Jebusites and it became the city of God! There is always hope, for God can change anyone or any place!

Lastly, any stronghold must be abiding: it must stand the test of time. **Only Jesus is all-permanent.** The mighty walls and towers of Babylon for years kept Babylon's enemies at bay, but in a night this mighty stronghold fell. (Daniel 5:30) The context of Nahum's burden (Nahum 1:1) was the seemingly impregnable fortress of Nineveh, the stronghold of the Assyrian Empire, but in the year 612 BC this stronghold ceased to exist. Hitler tried to build Fortress Europe, but on June 6, 1944 that mighty stronghold began to crumble. So it was with all the strongholds of the Anakims. Despite the fact Hebron was known for its construction and longevity (Genesis 23:2, Numbers 13:22, and Joshua 15:13) it too came to an end as a giant's city and a new Hebron rose out of the ashes. Every manmade stronghold built by man will eventually fall, even those constructed by 'giants'-would you not say the twin-towers were a mighty place build by amazing men and yet in just a few minutes they fell. Only Jesus Christ is the perfect stronghold, the best refuge and even 'the gates of hell' (Matthew 16:18) will not prevail against our stronghold. Jesus has stood the test of time, the attack from countless adversaries, and still to this day remains the best stronghold of them all.

It was Isaiah who gave the best description of a stronghold in my opinion, and the standard by which all strongholds should be judged: "For thou hast been a strength to the poor, a strength to the needy in his distress, a refuge from the storm, a shadow from the heat, when the blast of the 'terrible ones' is as a storm against a wall." (Isaiah 25:4) The Anakims thought that their strongholds built on the mountaintops of Canaan would allow them to remain in the land, to be a constant thorn in the side of the Israelites, yet they discovered that no such refuge existed for them because of the God of Joshua and Caleb!

19

HEBRON
THE CITADEL OF THE GIANTS

Numbers 13:22-And they ascended by the south, and came unto **HEBRON**; where **AHIMAN, SHESHAI, AND TALMAI, THE CHILDREN OF ANAK**, here. (Now **HEBRON** was built seven years before Zoan in Egypt.)

IF WE WERE TO name one place as the capital of the giants, it would have to be the mountain bastion of Hebron. As we have seen, this famous town was first built by the giant Arab, and named it after himself: "And the name of Hebron before was Kirjath-Arba (the city of Arba); which Arba was a great man among the Anakims." (Joshua 14:15) Could I interject a personal observation into this article before we continue? In 2010 I had a chance to travel to Israel with a study group from Dallas Theological Seminary. One of the disappointments of that trip was the fact we were not able to travel to Hebron (it is still on my bucket list) because there are still 'giants' in Hebron; oh, not men of great stature, but "the giant of terrorism": a growing evil in our modern world!

I found this geographical description of Hebron in Fausset's Bible Dictionary: "It is a picturesquely situated in a narrow valley nearly 3000 feet above sea level running from north to south (probably that of Eshcol, whence the spies got the great cluster of grapes-gigantic grapes for giants-Numbers 13:23)!" It is however my opinion that it was not for the grapes the 'giants' decided to settle in Hebron. For me, the roots of this giant citadel goes back to the purpose of Satan in his quest to resist the Divine Plan of God's people to possess the Promised Land and all the results of that conquest. Located very near to the heart of Hebron is the Machpelah Cave, the cemetery of the patriarchs. If Satan fought over the body of Moses: "Yet Michael the archangel when contending with the devil he disputed about the body of Moses......" (Jude 9 and Deuteronomy 34); then it is not beyond my interpretation that Satan would lay claim to the burial site of Abraham and his family? Death is something the Devil has always claimed as his own, despite the fact that it isn't (read carefully Hebrews 2:14–15 and Revelation 1:18). Why wouldn't he station three of his great giants near the spot of what he sees as some of his greatest victories: the death of the patriarchs! Cemeteries are the Devil's museums and mausoleums of his handwork in death, yet it is just his belief, not the truth!

By the time Abraham arrived in Canaan, the citadel of Hebron was already well established (Genesis 13:18). By the time Sarah died in Hebron (Genesis 23:2), the Hethites controlled the region (Genesis 23:10). Near Hebron was the field and cave where Abraham would bury his beloved. Interestingly to his day it is called El Khalil (the house of the friend of God) (James 2:23). After Sarah, Abraham was laid to rest in Machpelah by Isaac (Genesis 25:7–11; then Isaac and Rebekah (Genesis 35:27–29), as well as Jacob and Leah years latter (Genesis 49:31, 50:13). What better place to wait for the unfolding plan of God? Satan believed each and every time a man of God died that he was the cause. Had not Satan brought death to mankind through his temptation of Adam and Eve? I believe Satan has always seen the bodies of the saints as trophies of his greatest triumphs. If he couldn't have their souls; he would claim their bodies, and would place his 'giants' nearby to protect his property: dead men's bones (Matthew 23:27)!

Over the years between the death of Abraham and the arrival of Abraham's descendants, the giants spread out and took control of more than Hebron. Hebron was their capital but to that citadel they added the towns of Debir and Anab (Joshua 11:21). It is for this reason I believe that there were three giants named in our key verse printed above. One for each town: three fortified cities; three mighty giants, three more named warriors in Satan's army of super-soldiers. So to our list of Satan's Super Soldiers: Rephaim, Arba, Anak, Og, we must add the names of Ahiman, Sheshai, and Talmai. Interestingly, Ahiman means 'brother of man'; Sheshai means 'free or noble', and Talmai means 'bold or spirited'. Satan has always been good at labeling deadly giants with sweet sounding names. A good label doesn't change the fact that poison is in the bottle! These were the three leading 'giants' that were meet by God's giant killers in the contest for Hebron: a battle that gets as much press in the Bible as the battle against OG and the other giants of the East Bank. I am still asking myself why?

If Rephaim was the first giant and Anak was the feared giant and Arba was the future giant then the brothers three would be the fortress giants. What could be more frightening than a giant living in a castle? I remember well my first reading of John Bunyan's classic allegory "Pilgrim's Progress", and the Giant Despair in Doubting Castle! By the time Joshua and his armies had gotten to Hebron, Satan's Super Soldiers had locked themselves into what they thought were three impregnable citadels: Hebron, Debir, and Anab. I find it remarkable that the most powerful soldiers ever conceived had to find protection behind tall, thick walls setting on top of a mountain? Even Goliath was willing to fight in the open as was OG! I have come to the conclusion from my research on Biblical giants that the reason for this odd behavior was the fact the giants of Hebron had heard about the fate of their East Bank cousins. I came to this deduction after reading what Rahab said to the spies that came to her home in Jericho: "And she said unto them, I know that the Lord hath given you the land, and that your terror is fallen upon us, and all the inhabitants of the land (including the giants) faint because of you. For we have heard how the Lord dried up the water of the Red Sea for you, when ye came out of Egypt; and what ye did unto the two kings of Amorites, that were on the other side of Jordan, Sihon and OG, whom ye utterly destroyed. And as soon as we had heard these things, our hearts did melt, neither did there remain any more courage in any man (including the giants), because of you: for the Lord your God, He is God in heaven above, and in earth beneath." (Joshua 2:9–11) The feared giants (Numbers 13:33) were now afraid!

As with Hebron and the other citadels of southern Canaan, we too have three great 'giants' to face in our pilgrimage through this old world: sin, self, and Satan (our Ahiman, Sheshai, and Talmai). Read carefully I John 2:15–17 and you will find the three great locations of sin, self, and Satan: the lust of the flesh, the lust of the eyes, and the pride of life (our Hebron, Debir, and Anab). If you read Matthew 4:1–10, you will discover that these were the three places that Satan took Jesus to tempt Him. That like us (Hebrews 4:15), Jesus was confronted with these three 'giants' of wickedness and evil. For me, the three citadels of the three 'giants' are but a grand picture of how we too can defeat these strongholds and these strong soldiers of Satan. They should be afraid of us (I John 4:4), not we afraid of them (Matthew 10:28)! If we claim the spiritual weaponry that is our (II Corinthians 10:3–4) and put on the whole armor of God (Ephesians 6:10–18), we too can be victorious just like Joshua and Caleb and Othniel were. Three giant-killers for three giants are all that was required to defeat the fortress giants of Satan. We are never told how Hebron or her sister cities fell, just that they did fall in the assault lead by Joshua, Caleb, and Othniel. When the walls were breached was there a one-on-one battle like with David, we don't know. All the Bible tells us is that like with the former giants, Ahiman, Sheshai, and Talmai were all defeated and that the citadel fell to Caleb!

20

SHESHAI, AHIMAN, TALMAI
THE FORTRESS GIANTS

Joshua 15:14-And Caleb drove thence the three sons of Anak, **SHESHAI**, and **AHIMAN**, and **TALMAI** the children of Anak.

IT IS ONE THING to claim a mountain fortress filled with 'giants' (Joshua 14:12); it is an entirely different matter to actually conquer a mountain fortress filled with 'giants' (Joshua 14:14)! We will highlight Caleb, a true giant-killer, in a future article, but for this chapter in our book on Satan's Super Soldiers, we return for a closer look at the giants Caleb and Joshua and Othniel killed in the southern campaign for control of Canaan. I have come to believe that there is some spiritual significance illustrated by the fortress giants: Sheshai, Ahiman, and Talmai that will help us in our spiritual struggle against sin, self, and Satan himself!

The first giant was called **Sheshai** (free or noble). If this name had been given to a child of God we might think of the freedom that comes from the forgiveness of sin through the death of Jesus Christ (John 8:36) and the noble birth that is now ours through Him (I Peter 2:9). This cannot be the case when we are talking about a devilish creature like the giant Sheshai. What I believe Sheshai illustrates is the false 'freedom' Satan promotes to those that would listen. There is also a royal nobility preached by Satan's ministers (II Corinthians 11:13–15). In God's divine decision to give mankind the ability to choose, the freedom to make their own choices, free-will; mankind choose to do evil, transgress God's laws. In our chapter on the conditions of the world just before the flood where we located the first race of 'giants' (Genesis 6:4), we discovered that these 'giants' played a major role in the corrupting of the human race. Freedom of choose turned God's crowning creation into a wicked world. Along with this 'bent' to sin is the pride factor that can be traced back to Satan's days in Heaven. We learned in our last chapter that 'the pride of life' (I John 2:15) is one of the giants Satan uses to tempt man with. Noble pride is a satanic pride that was first found in the arrogance of Lucifer when he thought himself better than Jehovah, better than his Creator (Isaiah 14:12–15). The root of this wickedness was found in Satan and as death passed unto all men because of the sin of Adam (Romans 5:12), so pride has passed on to all of Satan's seed, including the 'giants'. Anak named his son 'noble', now there is a fleshly pride in a super-size, supernatural strength, and a satanic superiority in his boy. The sin of pride is one of the first transgressions we must conquer to this day if we are to successfully live the Christian life: "But He giveth more grace. Wherefore He saith, God resisteth the proud, but giveth grace unto the humble. Submit yourselves therefore to God. Resist the devil, and he will flee from you. Draw nigh to God, and He will draw nigh to you.... Humble yourselves in the sight of the Lord, and he will lift you up." (James 4:6–10) Like with Caleb, Sheshai will be your first fortress giant to slay, or he will slay you, just ask Nebuchadnezzar (Daniel 4:37)!

The second giant was called **Ahiman** (brother of man). We stated in our last chapter that we will face three great giants: sin, self, and Satan. If Sheshai is a symbol for the sin of pride, then Ahiman is the symbol for self, the enemy within! Once again if we were talking of a man of God named Ahiman (actually there was a Levite porter in the days of David named Ahiman-I Chronicles 9:17), we might speak of the connection with Jesus Christ to mankind as 'the Son of man', or the 'brother of man', but we are not writing of one of God's men, but one of Satan's Super Soldiers. We often speak of the brotherhood of Christians (I Peter 2:17), but what of the brotherhood of Satan: the link between demons and men. In my study of demonology, I have come to the conclusion that demons want to be men; that is why they love to possess men and women. They see themselves as brothers to mankind. To control a man is an ultimate pleasure for Satan's servants. Study carefully the cases of the demon-possessed in the New Testament, and you too will discover this link. 'The lust of the flesh', the second factor in the sin nature of Man is a great appeal to demons. Do you ever find a demon doing 'good' through someone they are possessing? In our debate over the creation of the race of 'giants', we shared with you the theory that they were the product of the sinful intercourse between demons and the daughters of men. One needs only go to the religious rituals of the inhabitants of Canaan to see the wicked sexual aspects of their rites and rituals, and as we have seen in our study of OG: the sin of fornication was used to corrupt the people of God after their defeat of OG. The giant was dead, but his philosophy and religion lived on and I am afraid lives on to this day. Like with Othniel, Ahiman (self) is an even harder giant to slay than pride!

The third giant was called **Talmai** (bold or spirited). Is there a better name for Satan than this? The Bible speaks of the boldness of Satan in the analogy of the 'lion' (I Peter 5:8). Is there anyone more spirited than Satan? He was the first spirit creature created by God. Once again, if we were writing of a man of God we might underline and highlight this concept with examples like Peter and John (Acts 4:13), or wonderful men like Timothy (I Timothy 1:7). Alas, we cannot because we are talking about an infamous instrument of Satan, a giant that was not only brazen but a perfect example of the Devil. If there is a sin that best describes the sin of Satan, it is 'the lust of the eyes'! The original sin was not pride; pride came after the sin of the lust of the eyes. Remember, Lucifer lifted up his eyes to see the glory of God and coveted that glory (Isaiah 14:13). The first sin that caused the fall of man was the lust of the eyes, when Eve looked at the fruit of the tree of the knowledge of good and evil and coveted that fruit. (Genesis 3:6) Satan used that same sin against Achan (Joshua 6–7) which delayed the advance of Israel into the Promised Land. Like with Joshua, Ahiman must be slain or it will eventually slay you!

I chose the verse printed above because of the word 'drove' that can be found in the text. In our next chapter we will see how the giant-killer Caleb and his son-in-law, Othniel, with Joshua's help kills the three fortress giants, but for us the best we can do with sin, self, and Satan is drive them; we can never kill them. There will never be a time we won't have to battle them, but we can drive them! As long as we live on this planet we will be hounded and harassed and haunted by all three. John warned us in his first epistle against those who through that after Christ's sacrifice we would no longer be able to sin (I John 1). Paul tells us of the ongoing battle with self in Galatians 5. And Satan at best will only leave us alone for a season or two (Luke 4:13); that he will be back. We are told to resist (James 4:7), or to hold back to drive back is all we are promised. Satan might flee and self might be suppressed and sin resisted, but they will be back eventually to tempt us again. Didn't Satan return to haunt Job for a second time (Job 1–2)? Didn't Satan return to tempt David again after Bathsheba (I Chronicles 21:1)? The good news is that we can continually 'drive' these three giants before us. If we would but keep on the attack we can drive them like a herd of cattle. Fortress giants are formidable in their massive defenses; they are furious in their defense, and they are fearsome in the wounds they can inflict, but like Caleb, Joshua, and Othniel we can defeat them if we "wholly follow the Lord" (Joshua 14:14). If we just say no, then our God will do the rest!

21

DEFEATING AHIMAN, SHESHAI, AND TALMAI

Judges 1:10-And Judah went against the Canaanites that dwelt in Hebron....and they **SLEW SHESHAI, AND AHIMAN, AND TALMAI.**

WHO KILLED THE GIANT Ahiman? Who killed the giant Sheshai? Who killed the giant Talmai? Consider this: Joshua 13:21 records that Joshua did; Joshua 15:14 records that Caleb did, and Judges 1:10 records that the men of Judah did (Othniel)! So who was ultimately responsible for the destruction of Satan's Super Soldiers of Hebron?

Most of us had never heard of General Norman Schwarzkopf until the Battle for Kuwait in 1991, but following that successful 100 hour war, his name has become a household word, both here in America and around the world. This precept of military fame has not changed since the first battlefield hero was revealed. Alexander was a boyish youth (just 20) from Macedonia, known only in Greece as the son and successor of a famous father (Phillip) when he marched his small army against the might of the Persian Empire. When he placed his phalanx (an organized group of spear and shield soldiers) in the center of the battlefield at Gaugamela he was better known, but after that battle he would forever be known as Alexander the Great. Darius, the king of most of the known world, had amassed the largest army the ancient world had ever seen to stop Alexander's march into the heart of his empire. Some say Darius had a million men on the field against Alexander's 40,000, but the number was probably nearer to 250,000. Despite being outnumbered five to one, or more, Alexander's army pulled off one of the biggest military upsets in history, and thereafter, he too was a household name. However sometimes the military heroes remain unknown: "There was a little city, and few men within it; and there came a great king against it, and besieged it, and built great bulwarks against it. Now there was found in it a poor wise man, and he by his wisdom delivered the city; yet no man remembered that same poor man." (Ecclesiastes 9:14–15) Could that have happened at Hebron, Debir, and Anak?

When we think of David and his giant battle, our mind more often than not goes back to a Sunday School class when we heard for the first time the famous encounter of David and Goliath. However, David's fight with the giant Philistine was only one of a number of memorable acts of bravery on the battlefield. Oh, he first became known for his courage in the army of Saul, but it was not until an unknown battle, the Battle in the Valley of Salt, does the Bible say David became famous in the world. "And David became famous after he returned from striking down eighteen thousand Edomites in the Valley of Salt." (II Samuel 8:13 NIV) Interestingly, the battle that made him universally famous was at the direct result of the skillful generalship and gallantry of three soldiers, not one! In I Chronicles 18:12, the credit for this victory is given to David's cousin, Abishai, one of David's mighty men (II Samuel 23:18–19). Then in Psalm 60, the recognition for the victory was given to another one of David's cousins, Joab; David 's chief of staff (II Samuel 8:16). Yet in II Samuel 8:13, David is given the glory for this victory; sound familiar, just like the diverse credit given at the Battle of Hebron and the defeat of Ahiman, Sheshai, and Talmai. Is there a pattern developing in Scripture?

Very rarely does one man win a major battle singlehandedly as David did at Elah. At the Battle of Gaugamela, Alexander was assisted mightily by Parmenion, who commanded the Thessalian cavalry on Alexander's left flank, and Philotas, who controlled half of the Macedonian archers and javelin men, as well as the Companion cavalry. It was Alexander's plan and glory, but it was the three men working in harmony together as a team that turned the Persian attack unto a rout. So it was at the Battle of Salt. Like Alexander, David was known for dividing his forces into parts (II Samuel 18:1–6), but when the smoke cleared it was David who got the glory as it was with Alexander. I have come to believe the same result happened at the Battle for Hebron and the defeat of the giant brothers. Joshua was the overall commander of the armies of Israel as David and Alexander were in their respective armies, but in particular Caleb was the captain of the army of Judah (the only living member of the first generation), and then there was Othniel (read carefully Judges 1:11–15) the foot soldier that was also involved. So it was the generalship of Joshua and the leadership of Caleb and the companionship of men like Othniel that eventually won the Battle of Hebron and the defeat of the 'giants'! I am convinced that Paul speaks of this concept in the spiritual battle in his first epistle to the Church at Corinth: "I have planted, Apollos watered; but God gave the increase. So then neither is he that planteth any thing, neither he that watereth; but God that giveth the increase. Now he that planteth and he that watereth are one: and every man shall receive his own reward according to his own labour. For we are labourers together with God....." (I Corinthians 3:6–9) Joshua planned, Caleb executed those plans, and Othniel fought!

So it is in the spiritual battles in life. It is Christ's plan, He is our Captain (Hebrews 2:10), but He shares the battlefield with others. If we are labourers together with Christ, we are also solders together with Christ (II Timothy 2:3–4). As the war is waged against great giants, we fight side by side sharing the toil and enduring the pain, but when the battle is over and won, we sing: "To God be the glory great things He has done!" It will be Christ's name and not our name, though we did the actual fighting, that will be honored. The Old King James version of the Bible uses this phrase in II Samuel 8:13: "....gat him a name...." Christ will gain fame, not the foot soldier, even if that foot soldier were a general. Today, we have a few Christians whose names are more recognized than Jesus' name; something is wrong! History in general has long forgotten Parmenion and Philotas and their part in the Battle of Gaugamela, but the fame of Alexander remains to this day. History has long forgotten the names of Abishai and Joab and their part in the Battle in the Valley of Salt, but David fame remains to this day. History has long forgotten Caleb and Othniel at the battle of the Three Giants (Hebron), but the fame of Joshua remains to this day. In the historical text and the Biblical text it is the Joshua (Jesus) that gets the credit, as it should be!

So it is when we become a soldier of Jesus Christ. Jeremiah gives God's advice to us: "Seekest thou great things of thyself? Seek them not!" (Jeremiah 45:5) Would you let me finish this chapter with the words of a favorite devotional writer, Gyln Evans found in his devotional "Daily with the King": "Seeking recognition and attention is characteristic of the world, not the disciple of Jesus Christ. Of course, some of God's servants do receive attention and renown, but the true servant will ignore such honor and strive to call attention to his Lord and Master. He will treat such fame not as an asset but a hindrance, so much 'refuse', (Philippians 2:8 NSRB) unless it enables him to glorify God. To serve God unnoticed takes sublime dedication. God is not looking for great men, but men who will allow Him to manifest Himself greatly in them. My chief end is to glorify God (not myself), and to enjoy Him (not a dazzling name) forever. May I never glory in my wisdom or strength, but in this: that I understand and know Him who is my God." Even if we kill a famous giant and go unrecognized!

22

CALEB'S PATIENCE IN BATTLING THE GIANTS

Joshua 15:13–14-And unto **CALEB** the son of Jephunneh he gave a part among the children of Judah, according to the commandment of the Lord to Joshua, even the city of Arba the father of Anak, which city is Hebron. And **CALEB** drove thence **THE THREE SONS OF ANAK, SHESHAI, AND AHI-MAN, AND TALMAI** the children of Anak.

HENRY WARD BEECHER TOLD of a woman who prayed for patience and God sent her a poor cook. Commenting on this, C. R. Findley writes, "The best answer to prayer may be the vision and strength to meet a circumstance or to assume a responsibility." No better definition describes what Caleb did at the Battle of Hebron, or the Battle of the Three Giants. What is interesting to me about this battle and its famous giant-killer is that Caleb waited 45 years (Joshua 14:10-"And now, behold, the Lord hath kept me alive, as He said, these _forty-five years_, even since the Lord spake this word unto Moses, while the children of Israel wandered in the wilderness: now, lo, I am this day fourscore and five years old.") to fight his battle against the 'giants'.

Caleb was about forty when he was chosen by Moses and God to spy out 'the promised land'. With eleven other (including Joshua-Numbers 13:1–16), he crossed into southern Canaan secretly from Kadash, "and they ascended by the south and came unto Hebron, where Ahiman, Sheshai, and Talmai, the children of Anak were." (Numbers 13:22) One of the first places Caleb observed in the land of promise was the mountaintop fortress city of Hebron, and for Caleb it was love at first sight. Despite seeing many more cities and wonderful places on their 40-day reconnaissance mission through the heartland of Canaan, no place captured Caleb's heart like Hebron. I think Caleb made a metal note in his mind to ask for Hebron when the land was disturbed to the people. Upon completing the spy mission, the twelve returning representatives of the tribes gave their report. However, there was not a unanimous report; the men were split on what to tell the people. The end results were two opinions on what should be done next.

Ten of the spies, scared by Anak's kids, discouraged the people and told them that the people were 'giants' (Numbers 13:33), the cities were fortresses, and the land devoured the inhabitants. Nevertheless, Caleb and Joshua, who had experienced everything the others had seen, gave a different observation and they "…..stilled the people before Moses and said, let us go up at once, and possess it, for we are well able to overcome it." (Numbers 13:30) But in the end God allowed the majority to rule (sometimes the majority in a democracy isn't right-sorry America), which resulted in over a forty year delay in Caleb's getting back to his beloved Hebron. Until a new generation could be trained, mostly the responsibility of Caleb and Joshua, Canaan would not be conquered and neither would Hebron; the 'giants' would remain in Caleb's city for a while longer. Caleb's desire to fight the 'giants' in their hilltop fortress would have to be put on hold for a more important battle; the battle for the minds and souls of Israel's next generation had to be fought, and in the process Caleb's patience would be tested.

In every aspect of life patience is needed, so why should the spiritual struggle against 'giants' be any different? The Christian soldier must master the Christian grace of patience. James writes in his practical Christian living book: "Take, my brethren, the prophets, who have spoken in the name of the Lord, for an example of suffering affliction, and of patience. Behold, we count them happy which endure." (James 5:10–11) Caleb had to endure months and years of aimless wandering before he even got another glimpse at Hebron. What patience he must have had to never lose sight of the site that kept him focused; to never lose sight of the goal of his life. The Bible tells us to admire the patience of Job (James 5:11), but I also admire the patience of Caleb. At forty, he was fit and strong and brave and ready to face the 'giants'; ready, willing, and able to take on the gigantic triplets of Hebron, but with each passing year of wandering he must have wondered?

He turned 50, then 60, and then 70 on a journey around and around the deserts of southern Canaan. As the children of Israel worked their way up the east bank of the Dead Sea for an assault on Jericho Caleb turned 80, and during the conquest of central and northern Canaan as he helped others conquer their promised land Caleb turned 85. And when Caleb's time had finally come, he was able to say: "And, lo, I am this day fourscore and five years old (85). As yet I am as strong this day as I was in the day that Moses sent me; as my strength was then, even so is my strength now, for war, both to go out and to come in." (Joshua 14:10–11) Patience doesn't weaken us, it strengthens us. Paul spoke of this I believe when he wrote to the Christians at Corinth: "For which cause we faint not (having patience) but though our outward man perish, yet this inward man is renewed day by day." (II Corinthians 4:16)

Caleb endured through patience because he never forgot God's promise to him: "Now therefore give me this mountain, where of the Lord spake in that day; for thou hearest in that day how the Anakims were there, and that the cities were great and fenced: if so be the Lord will be with me, then I shall be able to drive them out, AS HE LORD SAID!" (Joshua 14:12) Patience takes trusting the promises of God. Patience takes trusting the power of God. Patience relies on the presence of God through the waiting process. Patience is trusting that God will keep you and continue to strengthen you even when time passes and the aging process advances. Patience is trusting that even when it takes 45 years you will not lose your desire to take on the 'giants' hold up in your promised city. Paul told us: "For whatsoever things were written (including the story of Caleb) aforetime were written for our learning, that we through PATIENCE and comfort of the scriptures might have hope." (Romans 15:4) What promised goal haven't you reached yet? It is a godly patience that will get you through those seemingly endless years of hopelessness, for it is patience that gives us hope!

To Caleb, hope was spelled H-E-B-R-O-N. He kept its image before him as he marched around the Sinai desert training and instructing the next generation of soldiers as his old comrades died off one by one. In his mind eye he could still see Hebron as he fought the early battles for Canaan. Remember, only 40 years was he in the deserts, we forget it took at least five years to secure the bulk of the Promised Land and still there was much to conquer (Joshua 13). Caleb was patient enough to put his fight with the 'giants' on hold while he helped his brethren conquer. Only a patient man can: "Look not every man on his own things, but every man also on the things of others." (Philippians 2:4) Caleb fought in the east bank battles that won the lands of Gad and Rueben and the half tribe of Manasseh, including the battle with OG. He marched with the children of Israel around Jericho, and no doubt fought in the final battle against Ai. And then there was the battle of Gibeon and Hazor and no doubt countless others unnamed battles. At least five years of hard fighting and campaigning to defeat all the major Canaanite powers, and still Caleb's battle with the 'giants' of Hebron was before him. We too must learn patience in our war with the 'giants' of this age, but when the time is right we will be ready, well and by God's grace able to defeat 'giants'!

23

CALEB
THE GIANT KILLER

Joshua 14:13-And Joshua blessed him, and gave unto **CALEB** the son of Jephunneh Hebron for an inheritance.

As CALEB'S VICTORIES MOUNTED up during the battles for Canaan, his faith soared; until, the mountain full of 'giants' and the fortress full of titans couldn't diminish his confidence in the promises and power of His God. Patience is not a waiting time but a preparation time; a time for strengthening your faith and developing your skills for the battle against the giant that is in your inheritance. Only God knows of the courage it takes to conquer a mountain stronghold occupied by 'giants'. How often has the young soldier of Christ full of youthful courage and strength forgotten that experience is also a necessity? God often delays our major battles until we are ready and experienced enough to handle them. Impatience can be a deadly vice in battling a giant. Let us never forget that patience and preparation are just as important as participation!

It is interesting to me that the preparation for the Battle of Hebron is given more space in the Word of God than the actual battle: "From Hebron Caleb drove out the three Anakims-Sheshai, Ahiman, and Talmai, descendants of Anak." (Joshua 15:14 NIV) A battle that had been put off for 45 years has been given only one verse in the Bible!!! How could something that seems impossible be accomplished so easily? How could a battle that containing the greatest concentration of 'giants' in any Biblical story be over almost before it began? Sometimes our most feared battles turn out to be our easiest battles, if we simply wait with patience the timing of the Lord.

The city of Arba, a warrior of remarkable stature, was called Kirjath Arba, a city built seven years before the ancient and important Egyptian city of Zoan. (Numbers 13:22) However, the reason for its recapture goes back long before Caleb first set eyes on the impressive site. We often forget that Hebron was the burial site of the patriarchs: Abraham (Genesis 25:7–10), Isaac (Genesis 35:27–29), and Jacob (Genesis 50:12–13) were all buried in a cave just outside Hebron with their wives: Sarah, Rebekah, and Leah. It can be easily seen why Satan would located a regiment of his super soldiers there. As we have seen, if Satan would fight over the body of Moses (Jude 9), then he might see the bodies of the patriarchs as his trophies as well. We should never forget that the body is all Satan can claim, and Satan seems to get quite jealous over what he sees as his possession. I have come to believe that Caleb fought against the 'giants' of Hebron for the same reason David fought against Goliath; for the name and honor of his God, and though occupied by Satan's super soldiers for centuries, that sacred land needed to be liberated. We serve a patient God (Romans 15:4), a longsuffering God (II Peter 3:9), but God never forgets and He too is jealous over what is His. Remember, God will never ask us to do anything that He Himself will not do, so as He was patient, so Caleb was patient and they both waited the right time to attack, and when it was time a giant killer emerged.

We would do well as soldiers of Christ (II Timothy 2:3–4) to add to our spiritual armor the grace of patience. Peter exhorts us to add it in his second epistle: "And beside this, giving all diligence, add to your faith virtue, and to virtue knowledge, and to knowledge temperance, and to temperance patience….." (II Peter 1:5–6) Paul encourages us in his letter to the Hebrews: "….And let us run with patience the race that is set before us." (Hebrews 12:1) If we need such an example could I once again point you to Caleb and the Battle for Hebron? His was a 45 year race through long days and nights were patience was his only companion. Someone has said, **"That the stops of a good man are as ordered by the Lord as his steps!"** It is during those stops that patience is needed even when you feel that you are ready to face your giant. Without patience you will never be a giant-killer. Without perseverance you will never get to the top of your mountain filled with giants. It might take time, but with the Lord on your side your time will come!

Perhaps, this chapter is being read today by someone who sees life as having passed them by. Maybe, you have reached retirement age and haven't felt like you have reached your mountain-peak as yet? Just imagine Caleb's story if he had given up at age 65, as many Americans are doing today. Life isn't over at 65; it might just be getting starting? This is meaningful to me because at the writing of this chapter I am 65 (73 at the final editing). I have always liked what Paul Van Gorder once put in an Our Daily Bread article, and I quote: "The great Italian Violinist Nicol Paganini (1782–1840) willed his fine instrument to his home city of Genoa. His bequest carried one condition. The violin was never to be played; it would simply be placed on display. But that's not good for a finely crafted stringed instrument. It needed to be used and handed regularly if its beauty and value was to be retained. As a result of Paganini's request, his marvellous violin has become nothing more than a decaying piece of wood and string. It has wasted away as a museum piece. The principle of rejuvenation through usage also applies to people. Remember Caleb? At 85 years of age he was still going strong. He didn't let the threat of advancing years slow him down. Instead, he realized that as long as he had strength and there was land to possess, it was his for the taking. So he got busy. With great confidence in the Lord, he claimed Hebron for his people by driving out the enemy.....Like Caleb, we need to stay active. When we put ourselves on the shelf, we lose our usefulness. Our work on earth is not done as long as God gives us breath. Yes, we slow down and must relax our pace, but there is always some 'mountain' to climb for the Lord. Become a prayer warrior. Take on a project for your church. Volunteer to help in whatsoever way you can. But don't become **A RETIRED RELIC**! 'Growing old but not retiring, for the battle still is on; going on without relenting, till the final victory's won.' Someone has said, '*We cannot avoid growing old, but we can avoid growing cold!*'"

M. R. DeHaan, Sr., a week before he died put his life in perspective when he said, "Patience adorns the woman, approves a man, is loved in a child, is praised in the young, and admired in an old man!" Caleb was such a man and that's why he was a famous giant-killer. Do others see this in you at your age? In our on-going quest to discover the qualifications of a 'giant-killer' in our study of Satan's Super Soldiers, I believe we have found another characteristic: patience. We need to add to 'be obedient', 'be responsible'. 'be faithful', 'be yourself', 'be confident', and now 'be patient'. James challenges us with this: "But let patience have her perfect work that ye may be perfect and entire, wanting nothing." (James 1:4) Many fight there giants too soon and lose, and it takes sometimes a life time to overcome that defeat if they ever do? When God's ready and He thinks you're ready He will give you your mountain full of 'giants', and the battle will be quick, for no giant has ever won against ' a giant-killer', Caleb is proof of that. **Remember: a giant killer has a faith that never wavers; a strength that never weakens; a blessing that is never wasted; a love that never wanes, and a hope that never wanders.** Caleb was such a man and that is why he is our first 'giant-killer' profiled in this book, but he is not the last for there was a young man who married his daughter that was also a 'giant-killer'!

24

OTHNIEL
THE GIANT KILLER

Joshua 15:15–17-And he (Caleb) went up thence to the inhabitants of Debir: and the name of Debir before was Kirjathsepher. And Caleb said, he that smiteth Kirjathsepher, and taketh it, to him will I give Achsah my daughter to wife. And **OTHNIEL**, the son of Kenaz, the brother of Caleb, took it: and he gave him Achsah his daughter to wife.

"AND WHEN THE CHILDREN of Israel cried unto the Lord, the Lord raised up a deliverer to the children of Israel, who delivered them, even **OTHNIEL**, the son of Kenaz, Caleb's brother." (Judges 3:9) Seemingly, out of the blue, from the unknown came Othniel to fight the great Mesopotamian king Chushanrishathaim (Judges 3:8), but not so, if you know your history of 'giants'! In God's history of Israel's famous 'judges', we have the divine precept of preparation illustrated in the life of Othniel. It was the great devotional writer A. B. Simpson that once wrote: **"God is preparing His heroes; and when opportunity comes, He can fit them into their place in a moment, and the world will wonder where they came from!"** Such was the case with the son-in-law of Caleb, the first giant-killer. Othniel was ready and able to meet Chushanrishathaim because of his preparation at the Battle of Kirjathsepher, another stronghold of the 'giants', and therefore, another giant killer.

Caleb, the great co-laborer with Joshua, was wrapping up his occupation of Hebron and its surrounding towns when he came up against the city of Debir. Like all the other hilltop fortresses the city of Debir had high-walls and giant residents! (Joshua 14:12–15) Each attack against each citadel was successful as the 85-year old veteran of the wilderness wandering led the way and the attack. Each city of 'giants' fell to Caleb and his brethren from the tribe of Judah because Caleb *"....wholly followed the Lord God of Israel."* (Joshua 14:14) However, when this man of God reached the gates of Debir, better known as Kirjathsepher (Judges 1:11), Caleb changes his tactics. "And Caleb said, I will give my daughter Achsah in marriage to the man who attacks and captures Kirjathsepher." (Judges 1:12 NIV) Could Caleb have attacked Kirjathsepher himself? Certainly he could! (Joshua 14:11) So then why didn't he? Answer-his plans in preparing the next generation to take over! Caleb knew his days in Hebron and Canaan were numbered (remember, he and Joshua were the only living remnants of the first generation of Jews that came out of Egypt) and his time was short. Caleb knew that future enemies would attack what had been conquered and that those future enemies (like Chushanrishathaim) would have to be faced and destroyed, but who would defeat them when Joshua and Caleb were gone? Who would have the strength and experience and courage and leadership to lead the children of Israel in the future fights with 'giants'? So while he could help, advice and train, Caleb would step aside and challenge a younger man to fight the fight at Kirjathsepher, so a giant killer became a mentor to a giant killer!

Each new generation lives with members of an older generation, but often the conflicts come when the older generation doesn't want to yield leadership to a younger generation. I had that experience when I was the younger generation and I am determined not to make the mistake of my parent's generation. Granted, a generation that has fought the good fight of faith, but have chosen to their last days, to go to their graves in positions they should have long ago trained others to take over. People in that position have forgotten the challenge by Paul to his mentored friend, Timothy, "And the things that thou hast heard of me among many witnesses, the same commit thou to faithful men, who shall be able to teach others also, Thou therefore endure hardness, as a good soldier of Jesus Christ." (II Timothy 2:2–3) Caleb knew of Paul's teaching long before Paul and he was determined that his young nephew would know how to face gigantic challenges (like an invasion by a Mesopotamian king) long before it happened.

I believe Caleb was doing just that when he challenged Othniel to take on Debir, for in the battle for Kirjathsepher Caleb was preparing Othniel for the battle against Chushanrishathaim!

Someone has said, **"To prepare is half of faith's victory!"** "And Othniel, the son of Kenaz, Caleb's younger brother, took it….." (Judges 1:13) Though the battle was probably not as simple as that, the results were! With confidence and Uncle Caleb's support, and the motivation of the lovely Achsah, Othniel won the Battle for Kirjathsepher, and laid the groundwork for greater victories in his future; when the fate of the entire nation was on the line. When President George Washington was addressing Congress on January 8, 1790, he said this: **"To be prepared for war is one of the most effectual means of preserving peace!"** A Biblical illustration of this precept is seen in these words about a future preparation: "And next to him was Jehozabad, and with him a hundred and fourscore thousand ready prepared for the war." (II Chronicles 17:18) The great tragedy of the Mesopotamian servitude was just that; Israel had forgotten, or at least most of Israel had forgotten to prepare for war. The author of the Book of Judges gives this explanation: "Only that the generations of the children of Israel might know, to teach them war, at least such as before knew nothing thereof." (Judges 3:2) As Othniel's generation forgot, Othniel never forgot the lessons of Caleb and His God taught him at the battle with the 'giants' of Debir. As his father-in-law prepared 45 years to face the 'giants' of Hebron, Othniel was also prepared for his greatest battle. Othniel learned from Caleb that even in life's 'last mile of the way', a battle might have to be fought and therefore you better be ready, and he was! Who would have led our men into battle during the First Gulf War if General Norman Schwarzkopf after the Vietnam War had stopped preparing for war? Would that war have only lasted six short weeks if Schwarzkopf had not prepared well? If Othniel had not prepared well the eight year reign of terror (Judges 3:8) might have lasted 80 years? But God's man, God's giant killer was ready, welling, and able to take on another 'giant' when his God called.

Earlier in this chapter we recorded a quote by A. B. Simpson, and in the context of that quote he also made this interesting challenge to the topic of Othniel: "Let the Holy Ghost prepare you, dear friend, by the discipline of life; and when the last finishing touch has been given to the marble, it will be easy for God to put it on the pedestal, and fit it into its niche. There is a day coming when, like Othniel, we, too, shall judge the nations, and rule and reign with Christ on the millennial earth. But ere that glorious day can be we must let God prepare us, as He did Othniel at Kirjathsepher, amid the trials of our present life, and the little victories, the significance of which, perhaps, we little dream. At least, let us be sure of this, and if the Holy Ghost has an Othniel ready, the Lord of heaven and earth has a throne prepared for Him." In our study of 'giants' we have been more focused on the precepts that might help us in our battles and we are learning from giant killers like Caleb and Othniel the simple tactics that will also help us. Surely we can see the lesson from Othniel is **"preparation"**, even when we don't know what we are preparing for. Little did Othniel know the day he took on the 'giants' of Debir that another gigantic foe would haunt his land, and that his God would call on him to defeat that giant?

25

GREATNESS IS NOT GEOGRAPHICAL

Joshua 14:12-Now therefore give me **THIS MOUNTAIN**, whereof the Lord spake in that day; for thou hearest in that day how **ANAKIMS** were great and fenced: if so be the Lord will be with me, then I shall be able to drive them out, as the Lord said.

How OFTEN HAVE WE thought that 'greatness is geographical'? Because a giant is born in a great city, where he finds great opportunities for advancement and success, to grow large both physically and politically: then that is the reason he becomes great? But in reality, greatness does not depend on location! When a twenty year old man by the name of Alexander marched out of an insignificant province of Macedonia there were those who probably said, "Can anyone great come out of Macedonia?" Yet before this Alexander was finished campaigning he would be known to this day as Alexander the Great of Macedonia. Most would have thought he surely had come from Athens, or Sparta, but greatness is not geographical. Let me underline and highlight this precept with a strange and obscure prophecy concerning the Christ. Perhaps, a prophecy you have long overlooked, but illustrates this concept we are trying to explain in this chapter on giants. "And He went and lived in a town called Nazareth. So was fulfilled what was said through the prophets: He will be called a Nazarene." (Matthew 2:23 NIV) Jesus was the greatest of them all, and yet He spent the bulk of his earthly life in a backwater, an insignificant village called Nazareth. I believe that Caleb never feared the 'giants' of Hebron because Caleb believed that greatness was not geographical!

People and places of greatness can be a problem only when we see them through carnal eyes. A spiritual man like Caleb can see through the geographical terrain (mountains), the architectural towers (high walls), and the physical tall (giants). Giant soldiers that dominate a city don't ensure that the city is impregnable. I was watching a YouTube video last night on the capture of what the world believed to be the greatest fort (Eben Emael) mankind has ever constructed. This Belgium fortress was captured by just threescore German paratroopers in just a day in 1940. Every invincible, impregnable invention of man has always fallen, and in most cases quite easily (you ought to check out just how the handful of men defeated Eben Emael; it will reminded you of Hebron)! Tall walls that surround a city don't guarantee that the city will not fall. A city located on the top of a mountain doesn't mean that city will not be captured by ordinary soldiers. The Devil has long advocated the precept of greatest is geographical, physiological, and architectural: an invincible location, a powerful body, a famous city. The 'giants' of Hebron were a combination of all three concepts, and yet an old man (85) defeated them!

Jeremiah 24 tells us of a very illuminating parable that illustrates this concept dramatically. The Lord showed Jeremiah two baskets of figs, one containing good figs, the other bad figs. What is interesting is the good figs represented the Jews taken into captivity by Nebuchadnezzar, and the bad figs represented the Jews left in Jerusalem. If greatness or godliness is geographical then the good figs ought to have been in Jerusalem and the bad figs should have been in Babylon (Jeremiah 24:1–5)! Babylon was an evil place (Genesis 11:9), whereas Jerusalem was the city of God. Yet the exploits of Daniel, Hananiah, Azariah, and Mishael come out of Babylon, not Jerusalem. These great men and others like them, Zerubbabel, Ezra, Nehemiah, Esther, and Mordecai, came from Babylon. Peter even ended his epistle with: "The Church that is at Babylon, elected together with you saluteth you." (I Peter 5:13) Yes, if God wills it there could even be a Church in Hell because greatness and godliness are not geographical!

The revival of Nineveh ought to be proof enough that God's blessings and leadings takes place on people no matter where they are located (Jonah 4). Let us never forget that Heaven produced a Satan (Isaiah 14), and earth produced a Christ (John 1:14). Dr. J. H. Jowett writes: "Our Lord Jesus

Christ lived thirty years amid the happenings of the little town of Nazareth. Little villages spell out their stories in small events. And He, the young Prince of Glory, was in the carpenter's shop. He moved amid humdrum tasks, petty cares, village gossip, trifling trade, and He was faithful in that which was least. If these smaller things in life afford such rich opportunity for the finest loyalty, all of our lives are wonderfully wealthy in possibilities and promise. Even though our house is furnished with commonplace it can be the house of the Lord all the days of our lives." Why, because godliness and goodness and greatness is not geographical. Often the immoral, ungodly, unrighteous live in the best and cleanest house in town while the moral, godly, and righteous live on the wrong side of town.

We live in a day when the so called wise men of our age say that the fault with man is his environment, his evolution. They have said it so long most people now believe the lie that greatness, goodness, and godliness are all geographical in nature. If this be true why did a dirty, dusty, no account town hold the Son of God for thirty years? Surely Jerusalem, Rome, or Alexandria would have been a more fitting place for the Eternal God? How often today we blame our parents, our place of upbringing, or our environment for our failures, faults, and foolish acts. The Devil made me do it, I am a product of my environment have been mankind's excuses for millennium! In reality Nazareth can be my highest heaven and Jerusalem my deepest hell. A manger can hold an eternal King and the richest palace in the land an infidel king. Nazareth can shelter the God of all creation, while the city of God can give sanctuary to a wicked Herod. Why has this principle long escaped the Biblical scholar? Why have we preachers failed to proclaim this wonderful truth? Why have we spent so much time talking of talent and town trying to convince ourselves that geography counts, when it makes no difference at all! Even one of Jesus' future disciples asked this pointed question when first hearing of Jesus: "Can any good thing come out of Nazareth?" (John 1:46)

This doctrine has also become the primary message of those that preach the 'social gospel'. The place is the problem, not the people in that place. The Bible teaches the very opposite and Caleb's fight with the 'giants' is just one lesson. To understand this teaching you must concentrate on the people of the story not the places. Ur produced an Abraham (one of the greatest men of the Bible), while Jerusalem produced a Manasseh (one of the wicked people in the Bible). Egypt produced a Moses, while Israel produced an Ahab. Need I illustrate this concept further? Read for yourself in the Biblical accounts or secular history and you too will conclude that greatness is not geographical! Nettie Rooker says: "When I am tempted to repine that such a lowly lot is mine, there comes to me a voice which saith, 'Mine were the streets of Nazareth'. So mean, so common and confined, and He the Monarch of mankind! Yet patiently He traveled those narrow streets of Nazareth. It may be I shall never rise to place or fame beneath the skies but walk in straitened ways till death narrow as street of Nazareth, but if though honor's arch I tread and there forget to bend my head, Ah, let me hear the voice which saith, 'Mine were the streets of Nazareth.'" The real giant of Hebron was Caleb, as the real giant of Nazareth was Jesus!

26

THE LAST REFUGE OF THE GIANTS

Joshua 11:22-There was none of the ANAKIMS left in the land of the children of Israel: only in Gaza, in Gath, and in Ashdod, there remained.

IT IS AMAZING TO me in this study of 'giants' that so little is mentioned of the 'giants' during the conquest of Canaan. The primary reason the children of Israel gave for not marching immediately into southern Canaan from Kadash were the 'giants' (Numbers 13:33), yet when it came to fighting the 'giants', the 'giants' seemed to offer little resistance! Joshua, almost in a passing fashion, notes that the 'giants' had been driven out of their strongholds (Joshua 11:21), and only 'a few' remained. Joshua would also record this in Joshua 17:15: "And Joshua answered them, If thou be a great people, then get thee up to the wood country, and cut down for thyself there in the land of the Perizzites AND OF THE GIANTS, if Mount Ephraim be too narrow for thee." The 'giants' had been driven out of their ancestral lands and were now located in a few isolated areas; only a remnant, only the last of their kind, yet they were not finished!

Now we can see more clearly the migration of the mighty men of Satan through the conquest of Joshua and his army. Starting with the tribes of 'giants' from the East Bank of the Jordan (Rephaims) and continuing with the Hebron 'giants' (Anakims), eventually Joshua had chased these ancient foes into two bastions, their two final sanctuaries: the valley of 'giants' (Joshua 18:16) and the land of the Philistines (Joshua 11:22). I am convinced that these super soldiers were welcomed into these areas as refugees:

they became great mercenaries! Most forget that Joshua didn't control all the lands of Canaan after the conquest. Joshua's task was to make the land safe from war so that the tribes could finish the occupation of the land themselves. The mighty confederacies of nations had been defeated in battle. The mighty city-states had been conquered, and the great walled towns had fallen. Now there was to be a mopping up operation by the armies of the individual tribes (read carefully Judges 1). It was at this crossroad in Hebrew History that the 'giants' got another chance to regroup, relocate, rearm, and reproduce!

Instead of continuing the conquest, the individual tribes decided to try to co-existence with the undestroyed people groups of Canaan: "Neither did Manasseh drive out the inhabitants of Bethshean......And it came to pass, when Israel was strong, that they put the Canaanites to tribute, and did not utterly drive them out. Neither did Ephraim drive out the Canaanites that dwelt in Gezar......Neither did Zebulun drive out the inhabitants..... Neither did Asher drive out the inhabitants......Neither did Naphtali drive out the inhabitants......And the Amorites forced the children of Dan into the mountains: and they would not suffer them to come down into the valley......" (Judges 1:27–36) The tragedy of this appeasement by the tribes after the conquest was to lie before future generations of Jews many years (until the days of David-over 450 years-Acts 13:20) of difficult warfare. If they would have defeated and destroyed all these people groups as God had commanded, how much different might the history of Israel had been? For included among those that survived the first onslaught of the Army of Israel were the 'giants'. Like the other splinter groups, the 'giants' would be a thorn in the side of Israel all through the judge age and into the king age of Israel. How we need to learn this lesson! When God gives us a job to do we need to finish it, because if we don't we will leave to those who travel behind us a messy mess to clean up, if they can?

There have been a lot of battles in my Christian life that I should have never had to fight, but because of the failures in my life and the lives of others that have affected me, conquests unaccomplished, have resulted in unwarranted battles. Have you ever had to recapture lost territory in your life; territory you once controlled, but lost because you didn't finish the fight? Fighting twice certain battles of the mind or the flesh, when a good beating in the first fight would have settled the issue once and for all! The reason I have an understanding of the mistakes of the tribes in the early days of their settling into the land, I have also meet fellow comrades in the spiritual fight who have told me their 'war stories'. I once had a very good friend and a former parishioner who after many years captured and seemingly conquered his addiction to hard drink. For over ten years he was in control of that part of his life, seemingly a recovered alcoholic. All the signs pointed to a complete defeat of his ancient foe. His body became healthier, and so did his marriage and his relationship with his family. The Lord had granted him great grace to rule that part of his old life and kept it under control. Then in a moment of inattention and weakness, he yielded and opened the front gate of his heart and soul to the giant of drink to once again allow that devil to rule and reign in his life. A giant that he thought he had contained, a giant he thought he could co-exist with gained back everything he once controlled in his life. That was many, many years ago, and he has from that day been trying to recapture the sobriety he once enjoyed. Such are the modern facts of the 'giants' that survive to fight again; if you can't destroy them you better beware of them!

What battles are you re-fighting, or what territory are you trying to recapture in your life? What battles am I now fighting simply because someone in my past failed to secure the land? The Church of God is in a terrible struggle against forces that have reclaimed a piece of Christendom once fully under the control of Christianity. Just think of all the lands on this planet that we are sending missionaries back too, in order to simply reclaim what was once Christian! I have been often haunted by these two verses, one in Joshua and one in Judges, as I see the same thing happening in Christendom: "And Israel served the Lord all the days of Joshua, and all the days of the elders that outlived Joshua, and which had known all the works of the Lord, and that He had done for Israel." (Joshua 24:31) But then it says this: "And also all that generations were gathered unto their fathers, and there arose another generation after them, which knew not the Lord, nor yet the works which He had done for Israel." (Judges 2:10) There are parts of England and Scotland which a hundred years ago were conquered for Christ through the great revivals of Moody and Sankey. Scotland in the past has produced some of the greatest missionaries the Church has even seen and theologians beyond compare, yet in a trip to that fair land in 2003 I found the churches empty or closed and a pagan land like I found in 2006 in my first trip to India. I know missionaries in Scotland who are trying to recapture that land for Christ. What Happened? The giant Islam is stocking through the British Islands and Christianity seemingly has no power to stop it!

The sad truth about 'the last refuge of the giants' is that that refuge should have been conquered in the days of Joshua and not left to the days of David. The truth of the matter is that Joshua and his generation left the 'giants', so that another generation of Jews would have to deal with them. God had told them to completely eliminate the people of Canaan, including the 'giants' (Deuteronomy 7:1–5). If God's perfect will had been fulfilled I could have stopped my study of the 'giants' here and now, but as you will see I am only half way through this study of Satan's Super Soldiers!

27

GOLIATH
THE FAMOUS GIANT

I Samuel 17:4-And there went out a champion out of the camp of the Philistines named **GOLIATH**, of Gath, whose height was six cubits and a span.

SINCE THE ROUT OF the 'giants' in Hebron, the Bible has remained silent on Satan's Super Soldiers. As we learned, the 'giants' were not wiped out as God commanded, but a few escaped to find refuge in the land of the Philistines, and in the hill country of Ephraim; though these seem to have also died out over time for they are never mentioned again in Scripture. Throughout the 'age of the judges' (Acts 13:20) that lasted 450 years, we find no references to these super-human beings, but they continued on through 'the giant of Gath' (II Samuel 21:22) and would reappear during the kingships of Saul and David. Seemingly, out of nowhere and to the surprise of most, a giant stepped out on the battlefield of Elah (I Samuel 17:2) and that titan would go down in history as the most famous, if not the most infamous, giant of them all! I have come to believe that Goliath was from Anakim and not a Philistine, but the Philistines were always looking for a tactical edge on the battlefield, and when the 'giants' showed up they saw them not as a liability, but an asset. They trained them and equipped them for their fight against the invading Israelites. And thought we don't heard about them in Judges, we do read this: "And these are the nations which the Lord left, to prove Israel by them, even as many of Israel as had not known all the wars of Canaan......namely, the five lords of the Philistines....." (Judges 3:1, 2) The five lords of Philistia are Ashdod, Gaza, Askelon, Gath, and Ekron (I Samuel 6:17), and as we learned in our last chapter three of the five city-states held 'giants' (Joshua 11:22). I would start this section of our study of the latter day 'giants' with a short biography of Goliath because in the past we have only gotten a verse here or two verses there in Holy Writ, but this giant gets a whole chapter; there is something about this giant that God really wanted us to know.

Goliath comes from the Hebrew word 'golleh': **an exile**! This helps to explain the teaching that we have been highlighting and underlining in that Goliath's forefathers had been exiles from Hebron and refugees in the closing days of the conquest of Canaan (Joshua 11:21–22). There is a very interesting Hebrew legend that has come down through Jewish history of a connection between Goliath and Orpah, the daughter-in-law of Naomi. (Ruth 1) We are familiar with the history of the more famous daughter-in-law, Ruth, and her eventual marriage to Boaz (Ruth 2–4). The boy born to their union would be David's grandfather. The Bible doesn't tell us what happened to Orpah when she returned to Moab, but the legend says she became a harlot and produced four sons; all grew up to be giants. Her children were taunted with the saying: 'the son of a hundred fathers and one mother'. This eventually drove her children out of Moab where they became soldiers in the Army of Philistia where the offspring of Orpah and Ruth would stand face to face overlooking the battlefield at Elah? Was the giant of Gath, the grandson of Orpah? What a lesson that would teach about making the right chose at the crossroads of our life wouldn't it?

Goliath was the ultimate warrior of his day, at least, by any worldly standard of that day or now. What general wouldn't want this man in his army? He stood over nine feet high with an arsenal of state of the art weaponry (I Samuel 17:5–6). He was literally a walking tank. He had been a soldier from his youth (I Samuel 17:33) which no doubt made him a veteran of many a Philistine military campaign. He was experienced and arrogant which made him the ultimate intimidator. This giant from Gath singlehandedly frightened the entire army of Saul for forty day! Despite a huge reward for killing him, no Israelite soldier came forward to challenge this giant. Who would go up against his massive sword (I Samuel 17:51), his mighty spear (I Samuel 17:7), and his monstrous shield (I Samuel 17:41)? It would have been like attacking a fully armed and armored tank, especially when you add on his defensive weapons (I Samuel 17:5–6)! So for 40 days Saul and his generals debated and discussed their options, and all that time Goliath would daily stand in the Valley of Elah taunting Saul and his soldiers and blaspheming the God of Israel. Such is the case today with Satan's 'giants' in science, philosophy, and history. They boast of their mighty knowledge that they say can defeat any Biblical truth. They look and sound formable, but like Goliath they all have an Achilles heel!

Goliath's repeated challenges went unheeded until an unknown shepherd boy from Bethlehem happened to come into the camp by instruction from his father to visit his brothers who were fighting in Saul's army. David stepped forward that day and offered his services to the king and his God. At first his brothers (I Samuel 17:28) and then his king (I Samuel 17:33) were against it, but when no alternative could be found David marched off to war for the first time with a sling in one hand and a fist full of stones in the other (I Samuel 17:46) hand. His frail frame and short stature were laughed at by the mountain of a man from the Philistine camp. How we need to learn that despite our size, stature, or status, we are just the kind of people God is looking for to fight in His army and to take on Satan's Super Soldiers (I Corinthians 1:26–29)!

After Goliath cursed David's God (I Samuel 17:43–44), he prepared to finish off David quickly. With spear in hand he stepped forward to administer the coupe-le-grace with a sharp thrust from his huge spearhead. However, before Goliath could land the first blow, David had let loose a single stone from his sling. The stone's flight was sure and true, guided by God Himself. It landed in the one exposed areas on Goliath's forehead (I Samuel 17:49). The stone sunk deep and the giant Goliath didn't even know he had been hit. Stunned, Goliath staggered, the spear fell from his hand, and within a moment, as the two armies watched on opposite hills, Goliath fell as a giant Redwood tree would crash to the forest floor after being cut through. Lying motionless in the Valley of Elah, an eerie silence gripped both armies as David ran to Goliaths side, removed Goliath's sword from its sheath, he cut Goliath's head off (I Samuel 17:50–51). Today there might be a giant standing in your way. Stop looking at its size against your strength. Like David, put your trust in God and say: **"...the battle is the Lord's..."** (I Samuel 17:47)

If Rephaim was the first giant and Arba was the future giant and Og the final giant and Anak the feared giant and the brothers three of Hebron the fortress giants, then Goliath has to be the famous giant. His name has become one with the story of the 'giants' of the Bible. There would be many today that would be surprised by me naming the other 'giants', but you mention Goliath and mostly everybody would say I know him. The first truth I want you to see in the story of Goliath (others are coming) is that no matter how famous, or infamous, one of Satan's Super Soldiers becomes, their fame is fleeting at best. Goliath had built for himself a fierce reputation based on his size, his soldiering, and his spear. Remember, he was defeated by a shepherd boy with a sling and a stone. Granted, Goliath has become a favorite catch-word for something big, but it has also become the catch-word for memorial defeats over seemingly undefeatable foes; monumental wins over seemingly insurmountable odds. Goliath was really a wimp!!!!

28

THE GIANT PRIDE AT THE BATTLE OF ELAH

I Samuel 17:2-And Saul and the men of Israel were gathered together, and pitched by the Valley **ELAH**, and set the battle in array against the Philistines.

SOLOMON MIGHT NOT HAVE been speaking about 'giants' when he wrote: **"Pride goeth before destruction and a haughty spirit before a fall,"** (Proverbs 16:18) but a boastful, arrogant spirit came to the Battle of Elah, and a boastful and proud spirit can be the death of any soldier, physically as well as spiritually. A fitting example of this took place when the armies of King Saul of Israel and the armies of Philistia confounded each other in the Valley of Elah. Leading the army of the Philistines was a giant called Goliath, but he might as well been called "the Giant Pride".

Goliath entered the struggle at Elah with all the military advantages of his day. He was an experienced veteran (I Samuel 17:32); he was facing a frightened enemy (I Samuel 17:11); and he was bigger and better equipped than any other soldier on the field at Elah (I Samuel 17:4–7). Despite these assets, Goliath did carry a liability, pride! The world has long since changed the classification of this vice and its label: self-confidence is now the new label on this poison bottle. God has never changed the warning label, but the world now cheers the ingredients: cockiness, self-assertiveness, boastfulness, arrogant, and prideful. At the Battle of Elah Goliath was all this and more; he must have drunk the whole bottle, or he was just one of Satan's

Super Soldiers! "And he stood and cried unto the armies of Israel, and said unto them, why are ye come out to set your battle in array? Am I not a Philistine (sign of the Devil-John 8:44), and ye the servants of Saul? Choose you a man for you, and let him come down to me. If he be able to fight with me, and to kill me, then will we be your servants; but if I prevail against him, and kill him, then shall ye be our servants, and serve us. And the Philistine said, I defy the armies of Israel this day; give me a man, that we may fight together." (I Samuel 17:8–10) The challenge of pride is simply this: my stick is bigger and better than your stick and I can prove it if you test me. Pride in self and the ability of self is the most destructive pride of all.

Someone has said: **"A man can fracture his pride in a fall over his own bluff!"** I don't think Goliath was bluffing, he was boasting! Goliath not only boasted in his ability, but defied God to change what he thought to be a logical outcome of a one on one, a one-sided battle. David was the only man, even though he was the youngest there, who saw through Goliath's words when he drew this conclusion: "For who is this uncircumcised Philistine, that he should defy the armies of the living God?" (I Samuel 17:26) I like Moffatt's translation of Isaiah 16:6 describing the people of Moab, but Isaiah might just as well have been describing Goliath: **"They are so proud, so insolent, so haughty, so hollow, and so loud!"** John Ruskin writes: "In general, pride is at the bottom of all great mistakes. All the other passions do occasional good, but whenever pride puts in its word, everything goes wrong, and what it might be desirable to do quietly and innocently, it is morally dangerous to do proudly." Goliath never believed this at the Battle of Elah and it cost him his life at the hands of a boy from Bethlehem; how humiliating!

If what Goliath did for 40 days (I Samuel 17:16) isn't proof of his proud spirit, his encounter with David on the battlefield makes the doubter silent. "And when the Philistine looked about, and saw David, he disdained him: for he was but a youth, and ruddy, and of fair countenance." (I Samuel 17:42) Not only do proud people think themselves superior they also think that others are smaller, subpar, and silly compared to them. David was an insult to the arrogant attitude of Goliath. How could David be a worthy opponent for a man of Goliath's stature and superior military skills? The worst insult to Goliath's pride was a boy like David. If Samson had walked onto the battlefield that day, pride would have been flattered, but David was a child, a lad, a rookie at best a defenseless baby and pride got angry. If Saul, the tallest Israelite in the land, a head and a shoulder taller (I Samuel

9:2) than any other Jew in the land and the king of the land had walked out before Goliath, pride would have rejoiced, but David was a short kid, a mere speck in the eye of Goliath and pride went mad. If another titan had walked down the Valley of Elah to face Goliath, pride would have seen a worthy opponent at least, but even then pride would have boasted that his spear was bigger, or his sword was shaper, or this armor was better because pride can't help but feel superior, arrogant, and haughty!

"And the Philistine said unto David, am I a dog, that thou comest to me with staves? And the Philistine cured David's by his gods." (I Samuel 17:43) Recently at a Christian summer camp, I heard an interesting explanation of Goliath's reply to David concerning **"thou comest to me with staves?"** One of the counselors at Hampton Bible Camp in New Brunswick, Canada suggested that Goliath was referring to the staff David had in his hand (I Samuel 17:40), and that Goliath didn't notice the sling in David's other hand. Perhaps, David was hiding the sling and that when the stone was finally thrown Goliath didn't even see it coming because he was concentrating on the only weapon he thought David had? It appeared to Goliath that only a boy with a shepherd's rod was approaching him. Little did he know that one of the most dangerous weapons on the ancient battlefield was stocking him and a skilled, sniper, slinger had him dead in his sights! Whichever the case, once Goliath's wrath had been vented his pride returned with a prediction of death for David and a prideful attack on the character of David's faith in Jehovah.

"And the Philistine said to David, come to me, and I will give thy flesh unto the fowls of the air, and the beasts of the field." (I Samuel 17:44) Pride is a great false prophet. Pride will dramatically predict how matters will unfold, but in all of its existence pride has yet to prophecy any event correctly or successfully and the Battle of Elah was no exception to this rule or the precept that started this chapter! Paul gives us this revealing statement about pride: "For we command not ourselves against you, but give you occasion to glory on our behalf, that ye may have somewhat to answer them which glory in appearance, and not in heart."(II Corinthians 5:12) Moffatt's translates that last phrase this way: **"You are proud of externals instead of inward reality."** The New English Bible says: "Whose pride is all in outward show and not in inward worth." And Phillips paraphrase says: "Are so proud of the outward rather than the inward qualifications." As with Paul's answer, so too did David have an answer for the proudly Goliath.

"Then said David to the Philistine, thou comest to me with a sword, and with a spear, and with a shield; but I come to thee in the name of the Lord of Hosts, the God of the armies of Israel, whom thou hast defied." (I Samuel 17:45) David confronted pride with the only weapon that can defeat its gigantic arrogance, its monstrous insolence, its giant boasting: the name of God. James tells us: **"God resisteth the proud, but giveth grace unto the humble."** (James 4:6) Satan taught all his 'giants' pride because he is the father of it (I Timothy 3:6), but be assured that pride can be defeated by humility, and at the battle of Elah a humble shepherd boy taught an arrogant giant a few things about humility and a nation what it would take to be victorious over the new 'giants' on the block!

29

WHERE GOLIATH MADE HIS STAND

I Samuel 17:1, 3-Now the Philistines gathered together their armies to battle, and were gathered to gather at Shochoh, which belonged to Judah, and pitched between Shochoh and Azekah, in Ephesdammim....and the Philistines stood on a mountain on the one side, and Israel stood on a mountain on the other side: **and there was a valley between them.**

THE STAGE HAD BEEN set years ago when Moses confronted the Rephaims and Caleb faced off against the Anakims that another battle against the 'giants' would have to be fought; that is if there were still 'giants' in the Promised Land? What the forefathers of Saul had left, King Saul and his soldiers would have to face at the Battle of Elah (the valley located between the two armies-I Samuel 17:2-a valley I have seen from Azekah and what a thrill it was to see up close with my own eyes in 2010). Satan's 'giants' had a long memory (nearly 500 years between battles), and they sought revenge for the losses they suffered at the hands of the Israelites in the days of Joshua and Caleb. But why of all places did Goliath make his last stand in Elah.

Shochoh means 'hedge', but this belonged to Judah. Philistia had invaded and occupied a piece of the Promised Land. We sometimes miss the truth that it wasn't the armies of Saul attacking Philistia, but the Philistines attacked Israel. The root of this strike into the heart of Israel actually goes back to the days of the judges. The Philistines were just one of many people groups (Canaanites-Judges 4, Midianites-Judges 6 and a few others) God used that lived in the region to correct the wanderings and waywardness of the Jews. (Judges 13:1) The first attack of the Philistines into the Shephelah (low lands of southwestern Israel) is recorded in Judges 3:31; 400 years before the battle of Elah. During the judgeship of Samuel the Philistines were a constant and continual thorn in the side of the Israelites (I Samuel 4:1), and earlier in the kingship of Saul the Philistines had to be dealt with on numerous occasions (I Samuel 13:4), but now they were back and this time they had a super 'secret' weapon: arrogant, boastful, talented 'giants'. (II Samuel 21:22) There was no more surprised individual upon Goliath's first appearance than King Saul and his generals. How would they handle this new threat?

The armies (remember there were five city-states in Philistia: Ashdod, Gaza, Askelon, Ekron, and the primary home of the 'giants; Gath-I Samuel 6:17; with each mustering their own body of soldiers) gathered in Shochoh, but seemingly pitched their tents in Ephesdammim (boundary of blood-a fitting meaning). The title probably speaks volumes of the history of this location in relationship to the bitter feud between these two war-like people groups. Located between Shochoh (hedge) and Azekah (breach), this campsite was only a staging area for the confrontation between Saul's soldiers and Philistia warriors. For not far from Ephesdammim was the beautiful valley of Elah (oak) were the two massive armies would eventually face-off, but marching in the army of Gath was Goliath (and maybe his brothers?) and he would change this struggle between nations into a personal war, so why now? What was happening in Israel that would make the Philistines, and in particular the giant Goliath, bold enough to not only invade the Promised Land, but defy the God of that land (I Samuel 17:26) as well?

I am convinced in my study of the life of Saul that the Philistines had heard about the split between King Saul and the prophet Samuel (I Samuel 15). Samuel was no longer Saul's adviser, and the Philistines were a good student in remembering the power of Samuel. It was the prophet they feared because it was Samuel in the power of God that had chased them out of the land once before (I Samuel 7). Now that Samuel was out of the picture they would try again; perhaps, this time they could put the Israelites under tribute (taxes)? I also believe that it had gotten around that King Saul had grown melancholy (I Samuel 16). The king was having 'fits' and sometimes he went off his rocker and got a bit crazy; perhaps, King Saul was unfit to lead an army into battle. They had respected the strategic talent and warrior skill early on in King Saul's kingship and there was his brave and courageous son Jonathon that had beaten them on a number of occasion (I Samuel 13-14), but now the kingdom was in disarray; perhaps, this was the time to strike, and strike they did. When the combined might of Philistia was mustered, they marched on Israel hoping to get into the hill country through the Elah Valley. They would seek revenge for former defeats and hopefully gain some of their former glory back. Let us never forget that our enemies are also watching and waiting for a good time to strike when we have our guard down or are in disarray. Satan is looking for disharmony and any default or any division among us so that he can split us up and conquer us piece-meal. One of the best ways to prevent an attack by our foes is to stay unified, focused, and vigilant (I Peter 5:8). "Giants" love to attack when the advantage is all theirs and seemingly they thought they had a warrior that could lead them to victory!

I believe Goliath took his stand at Elah because he believed he could win. He sensed a defeated foe, and he was ready to strike. The first 40-days of the battle (I Samuel 17:21) seemed to prove Goliath's theory. But Goliath was a braggadocio that was brought down by a boy. How God loves to work this way. How many times in our study of 'giants' has the precepts of I Corinthians 1:26-29 come to light. God choses the weak to confront the strong; (David was weak physically but Goliath was strong.) God choses the ignorant to confront the wise; (David was ignorant in the ways of war and Goliath was smart.) God choses the base things to confront the proud; (David was seen as insignificant to Goliath while Goliath was proud and arrogant.) God choses the despised thing to confront the superior thing; (David was certainly despised even by his brothers and king and certainly by Goliath, but Goliath was superior in all things of the world.) and God choses the things that are not to confront the things that are! (David was certainly seen as nothing when he stepped onto the battle field at Elah and Goliath was the talk of both sides.) At the compiling of this chapter, I have just finished listening to a message by radio teacher David Jeremiah on his interpretation of I Corinthians 1:26-29. He titled his message **_The Nobility of God's Nobodies_**! What Goliath hadn't counted on was a 'nobody' coming to the fight. A nobody who would call his bluff and confront his pride!

The tragedy is not all prideful men are enemies of God, for some have been his servants; I am thinking of King Hezekiah (II Kings 20:13) when he opened his treasury to a few ambassadors from the far off country of Babylon. Trying to make himself something he was not, Hezekiah made a decision that cost his country and family dearly in the future. Because God is not a God who deals with sin differently, good or bad, righteous or unrighteous, He send his prophet Isaiah to pronounce judgment on Hezekiah (II Kings 20:17). Whether Hezekiah or Goliath, sometimes the stand you take isn't a good one because you take your stand against God and you will loss every time you take on God. More often than not God will use something or someone to humble your pride.

Galatians 6:7-Be not deceived: God is not mocked: for whatsoever a man soweth........

30

THE ARMAMENTS OF GOLIATH

I Samuel 17:5–7-And he (**GOLIATH**) had a helmet of brass upon his head, and he was armed with a coat of mail; and the weight of the coat was five thousand shekels of brass. And he had greaves of brass upon his legs and a target of brass between his shoulders. And the staff of his spear was like a weaver's beam; and his spears head weighted six hundred shekels of iron: and one bearing a shield went before him.

WE ALL KNOW ABOUT the Christian's weaponry described for us in Ephesians 6:10–18: a belt of truth, a breastplate of righteousness, boots of peace, a barrier of faith, a biretta of salvation, a Bible of scripture, and the battering ram of prayer, but what of Satan's weapons? When Goliath faced David on the battlefield of Elah, he was armed with some formable armaments. In this chapter on Satan's Super Soldiers, I would like to define and make a few spiritual observations on the different pieces of Goliath's garb:

1. HIS BODY HEIGHT-I Samuel 17:4. Even without his body armour, Goliath would have been a fearsome weapon. How big is the man that measures in at 'six cubits and a span'? It all depends on your definition of a 'cubit' and a 'span'. Goliath's height is actually unknown, but generally speaking, or at least according to those that study ancient measurements, a 'span' is half a cubit. So if we can define a 'cubit' we can come to a reasonable understanding of Goliath's stature. The word 'cubit' comes from a word that means 'lower arm'. So the general and

most accepted understanding of a cubit is the distance between the elbow and the middle finger: the lower arm. The problem that often arises is the fact that this measurement was taken at different times and usually the lower arm length of the curtain king of the land. Remember, at the time of this famous battle the king of the land was Saul and he was an exceptionally big man for his generation: a head and a shoulder taller than any in the land (I Samuel 9:2), thereby, making the cubit bigger than the average; which is 18 inches. I have seen the length from 16 to 22 inches, so how tall was Goliath: as short as 8 feet 6 inches, as tall as 12 feet 4 inches. He was probably somewhere in the middle, but no matter his height Goliath was of a prodigious size, a monstrous height, and a formable soldier. Satan has often use size to intimidate, and he has always despised the small (Zechariah 4:10), but as we know size doesn't mean anything to God!

2. HIS BRASS HELMET-I Samuel 17:5. Despite his size, Goliath seemed to be decked out with the latest in defensive armour. The description of Goliath's armament reads like 'what's' 'what's' of a Greek soldier of the day. Most believe the Philistines came from the Aegean Sea, so this shouldn't be surprising. I find it interesting that the very first piece of armor mention would eventually be his Achilles' heel, another Greek hero with a flaw! It was not a full head armament as we will see; which is in contrast to our 'helmet of salvation' (Ephesians 6:17) which is perfectly safe against all attacks (John 10:28–29)! Got your helmet on?

3. HIS BREATPLATE WEIGHT-I Samuel 17:5. Note, the most important article of armament the author wants us to see is 'the coat of mail'. In those days the breastplate was not a single piece of metal, but a series of small plates or rings hooked together like fish scales. The general definition of a shekel is 'half an ounce' which ment that Goliath's breastplate could have weighted up to 150 pounds! There are some who believe the author was trying to tell the value of 'the coat of mail' rather than the weight because 'shekel' was also used in weighing out the value of money. I think no matter what we decide, the author's description was clear: Goliath was armed with the best and most expensive weaponry of his day. Satan has a big expense account and he will always put the best he can muster on the field of battle. But remember, our Captain isn't cheap either, for he paid the greatest price of all to arm us when He died at the Battle of Calvary to win us out 'breastplate of righteousness' (Ephesians 6:14); ours was

'blood-bought' (I Corinthians 6:20 and II Corinthians 5:21) and more powerful.

4. HIS BRASS GREAVES-I Samuel 17:6. 'Greaves' are armor for the legs; usually from the ankle to the knee. Interestingly, Satan protected the legs while God protects the feet (Ephesians 6:15). My opinion why is found in Romans 10:15!

5. HIS BRASS TARGET-I Samuel 17:6. The Hebrew word for 'target' is 'kidon': javelin. This is the first offensive weapon mention by Samuel. Goliath's spear was for thrusting, but he also had a weapon to throw! Often placed between the shoulders, it could be easily reached and thrown. Goliath did have a weapon to reach David before David threw the stone, but it was never thrown, why?

6. HIS BIG SPEAR-I Samuel 17:7. In the days of Goliath the spear was the main battle weapon; a time when enemies like to fight it out at close range. The author wanted to impress us with the weight of the spear-head: 25 pounds! A weapon like that could cut a foe in two. Interestingly, the weight of the spear-head of another giant, Ishbibenob, was only half that weight (II Samuel 21:16). I believe it tells the size of the man that could wheeled such a spear. A formable weapon that came up against this precept of God: "No weapon that is formed against thee shall prosper…" (Isaiah 54:17) No not one, no matter the size, the power, the reach!

7. HIS BIG SHIELD-I Samuel 17:7. Because of the weight of all the weapons and the armor, Goliath was like most professional warriors of his day; he had an armourbearer to carry his shield and would only take it from the 'bearer' when the battle was imminent. They were round in those days and were created to protect the soldier from incoming objects like arrows and javelins and stones! What the helmet, breastplate, and greaves couldn't guard against the shield would? Often the javelin was thrown first with the free hand then the shield was taken up and the fight would be with shield and spear; if the spear broke then and only then would the warrior pick up his sword (Samuel 17:51). A weapon not even mentioned at first, but only added at the end of the battle. There is no indication that Goliath had taken the shield, for if he had he could have easily deflected the stone. The lesson for us is the importance of always having 'the shield of faith' (Ephesians 6:16) in hand; it does us no good in somebody else's hand!

These are the weapons mentioned in the description of Goliath's armaments. Certainly these weapons should have been sufficient to not only defend Goliath, but allowed him to take the offensive. I believe Paul highlights and underlines best the comparison and the reason Goliath's weapons failed him at the Battle of Elah: "For the weapons of our warfare are not carnal (the only weapons Goliath had), but mighty through God to the pulling down (or knocking down) of strong holds (and Goliath was that in all his armour)!" (II Corinthians 10:4) David came against Goliath with a sling and a stone, but we forget about his other weapons; weapons we will highlight in future chapters!

31

THE MASTER DUPLICATOR

I Samuel 17:8–10-And he (**GOLIATH**) stood and cried unto the armies of Israel, and said unto them, Why are ye come out to set your battle array? Am I not a Philistine, and ye servants to Saul? Choose you a man for you, and let him come down to me. If he be able to fight with me, and to kill me, then will we be your servants: but if I prevail against him, and kill him, then shall ye be our servants, and serve us. And the Philistine said, I defy the armies of Israel this day; give me a man, that we may fight together.

IN OUR LAST CHAPTER we listed the armor, the arsenal, and the armaments of the giant Goliath. Before we move on to the actual battle between the very special giant-killer God provided to defeat Goliath, I want you to notice an important tactic the Devil loves to deploy in the ongoing struggle between good and evil. We must understand and recognize that **Satan is a master duplicator**. Satan has the ability to reproduce, duplicate, the people and things God uses! The Devil has his imitations, his imitators, and they are artificial, but they appear to most as natural. God gave us the special spiritual arms to fight the good fight (Ephesians 6:10–18); the Devil armed Goliath with similar sounding arms (I Samuel 17:5–7). Satan has always been about the contest: his best against God's best. You need to recall the contest between Satan and God when God's champion (Job) was put up against Satan's fury (Job 1–2). Do you remember the contest in Egypt between God's men (Aaron and Moses) and Satan's men (Jannes and

Jambrees-II Timothy 3:8)? "....and Aaron cast down his rod before Pharaoh and it became a serpent. Then Pharaoh also called the wise men and the sorcerers......and they cast down every man his rod, and they became serpents, BUT AARON'S ROD SWALLOWED UP THEIR RODS." (Exodus 7:10-12 NIV) I believe what we have in this story of David and Goliath is another insightful illustration of the Devil's duplicates in action and defeat!

Satan is a crafty counterfeiter. God had his men in Pharaoh Palace (Moses and Aaron), but Satan had a couple of his men there as well (Jannes and Jambrees). Wherever there is a confrontation between right and wrong, it usually ends up in a contest between the Lord's champion or champions and Lucifer's champion or champions. In the very first book of the Bible (**Job not Genesis**-Genesis only gives a history of the past recorded by Moses; whereas, Job's story happened years before Moses wrote the Torah; probably in the days just before Abraham!), we get an insight into this eternal struggle between God and His first creation: the archangel Lucifer. In this story, Job was the battlefield, the object of conquest, and the ultimate prize. But Job taught us that the stumbling stones thrown in our path to check us, try us, and tempt us can become stepping stones to a 'Higher Ground' relationship with the Almighty. As we press on to that higher ground, we must be watchful and wary of the Devil's duplicates: Satan's champions! Whether Job's faith, David's sling, or Moses' rod, we might be outnumbered at times, out flanked, but we can never be outmatched with God on our side. Remember, Moses' rod that became a snake would devour the rods of Jannes and Jambrees that had become snakes; proving once and for all (did David remember his history as he took on Goliath) the superiority of God's originals over the Devil's counterfeits. These so called 'magicians of Egypt' would go on to duplicate water into blood, frogs in the land, but when Aaron hit the ground with the rod and it turned the dust into lice, the Bible says: "And the magicians did so with their enchantments to bring forth lice, BUT THEY COULD NOT....then the magicians said unto Pharaoh, This is **the finger of God**." (Exodus 8:18-19) Not only are the Devil's duplicated inferior, they are also limited! The Devil's wiles and giants are no match for the real thing, the genuine item, and they know it. Remember when Jesus confronted the 'Legion' of demons in Gergesenes (Mark 5:1-13)? No Contest! We need to relearn the precept taught to us by Jesus' brother: "Thou believest that there is one God, thou doest will, the devils also believe and tremble." (James 2:19)

Whether a false judge like Abimelech (Judges 9); a false prophet like Balaam (Numbers 22–24); a false Christian like Simeon (Acts 8); a false couple like Ananias and Sapphire (Acts 5); a false gospel like Paul describes (Galatians 1); a false Christ like the antichrist (I John 2); a false apostle like Judas (Luke 22); false magicians like Jannes and Jambrees (II Timothy 3), or a false armament and false statements like Goliath, Satan will duplicate anything or any position or any person to confront God's man! God wrote the Bible (II Peter 1:21), so Satan had to write a few: like the Books of Mormon and the Books of Islam to name two! God's explanation on how the world began is stated clearly in the Creation Story (Genesis 1–2), so Satan had to have a version and it is called 'evolution'! You name it, the Devil has a duplicate for; that is why we must hear and heed this stark warning from the pen of Paul: **"For such men are false apostles, deceitful workers, masquerading as apostles of Christ. And no wonder, for Satan himself masquerades as an angel of light. It is not surprising, then, if his servants masquerade as servants of righteousness."** (II Corinthians 11:13–15 NIV) God had a champion in the wings at Elah and Satan was ready with his champion, why else would Goliath challenge the armies of Saul the way he did? And as for me, another characteristic of Satan that comes out of Goliath's statement is his acknowledgment as being a Philistine, liar (John 8:44)! Goliath was no Philistine; he was an Anakin as we have seen in our trace of his roots and lineage; he was of his father the Devil, a liar too!

We do have a powerful and crafty adversary in the fallen angel Lucifer, but the best he can do is counterfeit. The Devil has never come up with an original idea or an original concept and he has never produced a real thing. I am amazed today that just how good the creators of the artificial have become. At a distance I have been fooled by artificial flowers, trees, you name it; they are very good, but once you get closer and touch or smell, the artificial loses every time to the real. Paul tells us to "Test everything. Hold on to the good." (I Thessalonians 5:21 NIV) We must use similar tactics against the Devil's best, and we all know that whether a dollar bill or a lily, no counterfeit can compare, or stand up to the real thing! I am convinced that was the difference between the soldiers of Saul and David. From a distance Goliath seemed invincible, but once David got close the fight was over in a moment. John told the believers of his century that many 'deceivers' (II John 7) had gone out into the world and that they needed to "Try the spirits to see if they are of God…" (I John 4:1) If we try them like David did they will be found wanting!

If you want something that is genuine and eternal you must come to the source of all that is real and right, the Lord Jesus Christ (John 1:1–3). If you are not careful, however, you will be fooled by one of Satan's counterfeits and will be fooled into fearing one of Satan's Supers Soldiers, just like Saul and his soldiers! (I Samuel 17:11) Don't be intimidated by the size of his shield, the strength of his spear, or the stature of the soldier. For 40 days Goliath fooled the men of God that he was superior, and then came along a shepherd boy who saw through the trickery, the mirage, the fakery, the counterfeit and realized that he was simply dealing with one of Satan's greatest duplicates!

32

GOD'S WEAPON VERSES SATAN'S WARRIOR

I Samuel 17:11–12-When Saul and all Israel heard those words of **THE PHILISTINE**; they were dismayed, and greatly afraid. Now **DAVID** was the son of that Ephrathite of Bethlehem-Judah, whose name was Jesse; and he had eight sons . . .

WHEN WILL MEN OF war and men who make war, including giant warriors, ever learn these two divine precept: **"Not by might, nor by power, but by my Spirit saith the Lord of Host,"** (Zechariah 4:6) and *"... The battle is the Lord's...."* (I Samuel 17:47) Since the earliest chapters in Genesis warfare between nations (Genesis 14) has been going on and continues on to this day (the Hamas/Israeli and Ukraine/Russia Wars as I edit this chapter), and despite the statements of men to the contrary, will go on until the end of times for this planet as it is prophesied (Revelation 20) in the Revelation! Despite the lesson learned many times over, that war never ends war, (In the history books we are told of 'the war that would end all wars' (World War 1), yet within 21 years the world was at war again-World War 2), the warriors of the world still think that a better weapon, or a better warrior is the ultimate answer to human conflict (how has the atomic bomb, the ultimate weapon, worked out?). The nations of this planet are still spending trillions annually to improve weaponry and the lethalness of the warrior. The movie makers have fueled this lunacy by creating a series of seemingly invincible warriors with unlimited weapons. Years ago I was fascinated by a character called 'Rambo'; I still enjoy watching the series of films that came out over the years. Rambo isn't new, for in the days of the Battle of Elah he was called 'Goliath': a giant of a man who really lived and to whom his entire nation was willing to sacrifice its destiny on the ability of this warrior to beat anyone in 'one on one' combat (I Samuel 17:9)!

The 'duel' as it is known in ancient history was an interesting strategy used by many of the opposing armies of the Middle East. More often than not, it was a fight to the finish between selected champions from either side. David and Goliath might be the most famous Biblical example but they are not the only one. Second Samuel 2:12–17 records a mass 'duel' fought between 12 men of David's army and 12 men of Saul's (Saul was dead at this time but his son was still trying to hold onto the kingdom of his father against the forces of David) in which the duelist were all killed and a subsequent battle had to be fought, but under normal circumstances the conflict was waged between opposite opponents as in the case of Goliath of Gath and David of Bethlehem. This faceoff happened because of a seemingly old-fashion standoff that occurred when the Army of Philistia tried to invade the Shephelah (low hill country) of Israel. Because of the equal size of the armies and the hilly terrain neither side wanted to come off their high ground defensive line to fight in the valley: "And the Philistines stood on a mountain on the one side, and Israel stood on a mountain on the other side, and there was a valley between them." (I Samuel 17:3) I have been to see the Valley of Elah in the Shephelah in Israel, and for either side to attack the other would have been suicidal.

To break the impasse (David wouldn't even arrive at the battlefield until 40 days had passed in the standoff-I Samuel 17:16) the Philistines revealed their secret weapon: enter stage right Rambo's ancestor, a man tall in stature and armed to the teeth. Even if we take the shortest meaning of the word 'cubit', Goliath was at least 9 ½ feet tall and if we take the maximum Goliath could have been over 13 feet tall! Even when you put the wrestler Aundry the Giant or the basketball player Manuite Bol up against Goliath they would have been small, short cousins. If Goliath's size wasn't impressive enough there was that gleaming array of weaponry: armor over most of his body and what the armor didn't cover there was that massive shield. Then there were the javelin, the spear, and the sword, no doubt supersized to fit Goliath. There is some disagreement but most feel the armor and the armaments weighed between 200 and 300 pounds. Who did God have to stand up against this ultimate warrior and his supreme weapons?

God had promised His people: **"No weapon that is formed against thee shall prosper, and every tongue that shall rise against thee in judgment thou shalt condemn."** (Isaiah 54: 17) Goliath is a great illustration of the truth found in this divine principle. Goliath's mistake at the battle of Elah was not so much his technique of fighting, but his tongue: "Then saith David to the Philistine, Thou comest to me with a sword, and with a spear and with a shield, but I come to thee in the name of the Lord of Hosts, the God of the armies of Israel, WHOM THOU HAST DEFIED." (I Samuel 17:45) For 40 days Goliath had taunted Saul and his soldiers, but he had also taunted the Lord (I Samuel 17:16). The last thing any moral man wants to do, even if you are a giant, is to challenge the Almighty to a contest, me against Him! For not only will He defeat you, He will humble you in the process and in such a contest God will not put a Titan up against your Giant, for as we have learned in our study of the 'giants': **"And God hath chosen the weak things of the world to confound the things which are mighty."** (I Corinthians 1:27) God doesn't even go to His heavenly army for a champion (the archangel Michael comes to mind-what a one-sided battle that would have been), but choses from the weak things of the world and that weak thing that day for God was a shepherd boy from Bethlehem named David!

Physically there was no comparison. Most feel at the time of the famous battle that David was barely a teenager, if he was even one (I think he was between 10–12)! *Professionally there was no comparison.* David might have been an experienced shepherd, but Goliath was a veteran soldier (I Samuel 17:35). *Offensively there was no comparison.* Goliath had an arsenal of well-developed weapons while David had a boy's slingshot! The Philistines didn't use the sling in combat (though there were a lot of ancient armies that did including the greatest army of the ancient world-Alexander the Great's army) thinking the weapon was useless in hand to hand combat which they preferred! So Goliath saw no threat when David showed up in the valley of Elah with a sling and stone. Some say three strikes and you are out, but that only applies to baseball not a battlefield. What Goliath couldn't see was what would eventually defeat him: 'the Spirit of the Lord' (Zechariah 4:6)! Philistia thought it had a secret weapon in Goliath, but it was David who stood on the battlefield with a secret weapon!

David would write these words after the Battle of Elah and I am convinced he was thinking of Goliath when he penned this famous song: "I have wounded them that they were not able to rise (remember the stone only knocked Goliath down; it was the sword of Goliath that killed him-I Samuel 17:51): they are fallen under my feet (I Samuel 17:49). For Thou hast girded me with strength unto the battle (I Samuel 17:46): Thou hast subdued under me those that rose up against me (I Samuel 17:50). Thou hast also given me the necks of mine enemies (I Samuel 17:51); that I might destroy them that hate me (I Samuel 17:42–43)!" (Psalm 18:38–40) The enemy never learns. They think with better weapons and bigger warrior's victory is sure. I don't know what giant is taunting you today; it matters not if '*the Spirit*' of God is on your side. As someone once said: **"We may face situations beyond our resources, but never beyond God's reserves!"**

33

WHAT MADE DAVID
A GIANT-KILLER?

I Samuel 17:15-But **DAVID** went and returned from Saul to feed his father's sheep in Bethlehem.

IF GOLIATH IS THE most famous of all the Biblical 'giants', then David is the most famous 'giant-killer' of the Scriptures, and we can learn a lot from this boy who killed one of Satan's Super Soldiers! In our chapters about 'giants', so far, we have highlighted and underlined seven characteristics of a 'giant-killer'. Did David possess these qualities; did David have the right stuff to take on a giant? I believe I can show you from David's encounter with Goliath that he did qualify in all seven areas to kill a giant. Let us notice again in the life of David these characteristics of a 'giant-killer':

1. **BE OBEDIENT.** I Samuel 17:17: "And Jesse said unto David his son, Take now for thy brethren an ephah of this parched corn, and these ten loaves, and run to the camp to thy brethren." The father said it, and David did it. David was so use to obeying his earthly father that when his heavenly Father spoke he also obeyed. (Ephesians 6:1) Giant-killers are not born, but trained. Our basic nature is to disobey, just like our first parents, but a child that is taught to obey will eventually obey father or Father! David knew how to obey orders long before he even knew of a Goliath, so when he came face to face with the giant he knew nothing but obedience. Is it any wonder that God had chosen

David to replace King Saul? (I Samuel 15:28) I would have you notice also Jesse's instruction to 'run' to his brothers, and David would also 'run' toward Goliath (I Samuel 17:48), for me a sign that David's was quick to obey; that in haste he obeyed father's orders!

2. **BE RESPONSIBLE.** I Samuel 17:20: "And David rose up early in the morning, and left the sheep with a keeper, and took, and went, as Jesse had commanded him; and he came to the trench, as the host was going forth to the fight, and shouted for battle." Before David left for the battlefront, he made such the sheep were taken care of at the homefront: *'left the sheep with a keeper'*! Some people think that a new command relieves them of their current or old responsibility. Not So! If we show responsibility in one area, God will give us responsibilities in other areas. This is the meaning of the parable of the 'talents' (Matthew 25:14–30). Once you show yourself trustworthy on the homefront, God will give you a responsibility on the battlefront! David could have gotten excited over the new assignment, but he never forgot his old assignment, do we?

3. **BE PATIENT.** I Samuel 17:28: "And Eliab his eldest brother heard when he spake unto the men; and Eliab's anger was kindled against David, and he said, Why camest thou down hither? And with whom hast thou left those few sheep in the wilderness? I know thy pride, and the naughtiness of thine heart; for thou art come down that thou mightiest see the battle." We sometimes forget before this battle that David had become King Saul's armourbearer (I Samuel 16:21)! Why did King Saul send David home before the big battle? (I Samuel 17:15) I have come to the conclusion King Saul thought David was too young (I Samuel 17:33) to fight at Elah. I think this shows David's patient spirit. No doubt he was upset to be sent home, but he waited on the Lord (Isaiah 40:31). David lived by God's timetable, and he knew the Lord timing was perfect, so he was patient!

4. **BE FAITHFUL.** I Samuel 17:35: "And I went out after him, and smote him, and delivered it out of his mouth: and when he rose against me, I caught him by his beard, and smote him, and slew him." David was faithful in defending his father's flock from an Asiatic bear, a very aggressive creature, and an Asiatic lion, the king of the beast (Proverbs 30:30), so this set the stage for David's willingness to defend the Army of the Lord (I Corinthians 4:2). Faithfulness is a key ingredient in any

'giant-killer'; whether in private, as David experienced in the fields of Bethlehem, or in public, as David would experience on the battlefield of Elah (Luke 19:17). Each small battle we find ourselves faithful is but a dress rehearsal for a bigger battle to come. Faithful against lions or against giant, all the same!

5. **BE YOURSELF.** I Samuel 17:39: "And David girded his sword upon his armour, and he assayed to go; for he had not proved it. And David said unto Saul, I cannot go with these; for I have not proved them, And David put them off him." Can you picture a man's armor on a boy's body? David was smart enough to know that he was no expert in wielding a sword, but he was confident in slinging a stone (Matthew 6:27).Whether bear or giant, the opponent might change but the weapon in the hand of the warriors stays the same (Ephesians 6:10–18). We must be who we are and what God has made and gifted us with and to trust in another man's gift or skill would be foolish. It is time we simple are who God created us to be! We have many in the army of the Lord putting up their 'shield of faith' for faith in medical funds, stocks and bond, and a bank account. We have just as many putting up the 'sword of the Spirit' to quote some philosopher, religious leader!

6. **BE PREPARED.** I Samuel 17:40: "And he took his staff in his hand, and chose him five smooth stones out of the brook, and put them in a shepherd's bag with he had, even in a scrip; and his sling was in his hand; and he drew near the Philistine." As with the unexpected attack of the lion and the bear, David was preforming his shepherd duties, but he was prepared to fight. David had come to Saul's camp to deliver some food to his brothers, but he was ready to fight. He hadn't left his sling at home! How many days had David carried his sling without using it, but on the day it was needed the sling was ready as was the slinger! Throughout the Bible we are challenged to be at the ready (II Timothy 2:21 and 3:17), and note these verses are in the context of the Christian warrior (II Timothy 2:3–4). One of the greatest causes of defeat in Christendom today is the lack of preparedness. If we are not fighting we ought to be preparing to fight!

7. **BE CONFIDENT.** I Samuel 17:46: "This day will the Lord deliver thee into mine hand; and I will smite thee....." Every soldier in Saul's army, including Saul himself, saw Goliath as to big to fight, while David saw

Goliath as to big to miss! Courage comes with confidence, and David had put his confidence in his Lord: "And all this assembly shall know that the Lord saveth not with sword and spear: for the battle is the Lord's, and he will give you into our hands." (I Samuel 17:47) David had learned, been taught to trust in the Lord God of Israel in every situation and circumstance of his life. And while it was hard for David's older brother and David's king to understand David's belief that he could with God's help defeat the giant, David had no doubts. What Eliab saw as pride (I Samuel 17:28) and King Saul saw as inexperience (I Samuel 17:33), David saw as confidence in a cause (I Samuel 17:29). We too can develop such confidence if we trust in Jesus.

34

DAVID
THE GIANT-KILLER

I Samuel 17:51-Therefore David ran, and stood upon the Philistine, and took his
sword, and drew it out of the sheath thereof, and slew him, and cut off his head
therewith. And when the Philistines saw their champion was dead, they fled.

THE BATTLE OF ELAH was almost never fought (I Samuel 17:3). A stalemate
had occurred because of the terrain and the balance of forces. For either
side to attack the other through the Valley of Elah would immediately give
the advantage to the force still holding the high ground. Generals have
discovered over time that it is a very difficult maneuver to attack uphill.
It takes more men, more time, with more military skill to defeat a foe who
is entrenched (I Samuel 17:20) on a hill, a mountain, a bluff, or any high
ground higher than the attacking force. Saul was willing to wait for the Philistines to attack his position, and seemingly the Philistines were willing to
wait for the Israelites to attack their fortified position. The stalemate lasted
forty days (I Samuel 17:16). However, during that period the Israelites were
taunted from the valley floor by the giant Goliath. Even in the valley the
Israelites saw Goliath as a giant; an invincible, incredible foe with weaponry
that could defeat any weapon they had. Did Israel have a champion?

Goliath proposed daily a simple one on one fight between him and a
man of their choosing. The winner of the mini-war would win the battle
and the losing nation would submit to the winning nation, but "when Saul

and all Israel heard those words of the Philistine, they were dismayed and greatly afraid." (I Samuel 17:11) As we have noted in other chapters: the logical and most reasonable opponent for Goliath was King Saul who stood "a head taller than any of the others." (I Samuel 9:2 NIV) Though not as big as the giant, Saul was the biggest Israelite, and Israel's most noteworthy warrior by experience and reputation (I Samuel 9–15)! Nevertheless, Saul refused to pick up the gauntlet of Goliath and instead offered a huge reward for anybody that would (I Samuel 17:25); there seemingly were no takers! Where was Israel's champion?

For almost six weeks Goliath taunted and haunted Saul and his soldiers every morning with the same challenge, and for almost a month and a half the reward went unclaimed! The standoff seemed destined to continue into another day, another week, another month until on the 40th day a young shepherd-boy from Bethlehem walk into Saul's fortified camp with some food for his three brothers who were fighting in Saul's army. (I Samuel 17:12–20) There does appear that some clashes had happened between the two armies before David arrived (I Samuel 17:21, 24), but no outcome had been determined by these encounters. As the story is told David's arrival coincided with Goliath's daily challenge and rebuke of King Saul and his God. When David heard the giant's blasphemy and boasting he became furious and said boldly: "For who is this uncircumcised Philistine, that he should defy the armies of the Living God?" (I Samuel 17:26) David's spiritual indignation stirred him to wonder why nobody was defending the reputation and the name of the Lord God of Hosts. Was this Israel's champion?

David immediately offered his services to King Saul to go out and fight Goliath (I Samuel 17:32). Saul at first rejected the offer by concluding: "You are not able to go out against the Philistine and fight him, you are only a boy, and he has been a fighting man from his youth." (I Samuel 17:33 NIV) From a military standpoint it was a logical deduction, and secretly King Saul loved David as a son (I Samuel 16:21) and he feared for David's life. David on the other hand would hear nothing of Saul's logic or reason, but shared with his king some of his own logic and reason. He told the king of two occasions when he had simply trusted in God, and his Lord had delivered him from the paw of a lion and the paw of a bear (I Samuel 17:34–37). David's logic was if God could do that for him in the pasturelands around his father's farm in Bethlehem, then certainly the Lord could do the same for him on the battlefield of Elah! As with the lion and the bear, then why not with Goliath? David had learned at a very early age what so many today fail to learn into adulthood: though one's foes come in a variety of shapes and sizes, all are still at the mercy of God and God's man, or boy, no matter how ferocious, how fearful, or how formidable they may appear. Israel had a champion!

Finally, King Saul gave in to David's argument and reasoning. It was then that King Saul again stepped into the debate how best to defeat the giant. Saul tried to outfit David for the fight by putting his young armour-bearer into his own armor (I Samuel 17:38–39). So often the natural man only sees the natural foe, when in reality the real enemy is not what we see, but what is not seen. Paul wrote of this concept in Ephesians 6:12–14: "For we wrestle not against flesh and blood, but against principalities, against powers, against spiritual rulers of darkness in this world, against spiritual wickedness in high places. Wherefore take unto you the whole armour of God, that ye may be able to with stand in the evil day, and having done all to stand. Stand......" I have come to believe as David felt the weight of the armour he came to the conclusion that this wasn't the armor that had protected him from the lion and the bear. I believe he deducted that God's armour was better than man's armour and that he would trust in God for his protection (I Samuel 17:39). When will we ever learn not to trust in man's devices in the spiritual battle we are in? I am afraid like Saul we have so long used man's weapons we have forgotten the power of God's weaponry (II Corinthians 10:4)! It is time we practice using God's arsenal instead of the world's armaments. David's would pen this in one of his beloved psalms: "Some trust in chariots, and some in horses, but we will remember the name of the Lord our God." (Psalm 20:7) A truth he tested against a giant and found it to be trustworthy. It is hard to put down the things of the world for the things of the Word!

Most people who know 'the rest of the story' say David went up against the mighty Goliath with only a staff, a sting, and a handful of stones (I Samuel 17:40). I have come to believe that David was also armored with "the belt of truth, the breastplate of righteousness, the footwear of peace, the shield of faith, a helmet of salvation, the sword of the Spirit, and prayer in the Spirit (Ephesians 6:14–18); unseen weaponry by some but David had put his trust in the unseen verses the seen. The other aspect of David's trust was mentioned in Psalm 20:7 and revealed in this statement just before David's let the stone fly: "Then said David to the Philistine, Thou comest to me with a sword, and with a spear, and with a shield: but I come to thee IN

THE NAME OF THE LORD OF HOSTS, the God of the armies of Israel, whom thou hast defied." (I Samuel 17:45) Can't you see David offering up a simple prayer in the name of his God? I have been studying again the psalms and I have come to believe that the prayer David might have prayed at Elah was either Psalm 31:15 or Psalm 41:2? You might find either psalm an interesting insight into the mind and the motives of a "giant-killer" on the battlefield of Elah.

So what makes a successful 'giant-killer', certainly the characteristics of our last chapter would be the qualification, but for me the best quality David showed against Goliath was his absolute trust and unmoving confidence in the God that he served!

35

DEEP INSIDE THE ARMOR
THE WARRIOR IS A CHILD

I Samuel 17:33-And Saul said to David, Thou art not able to go against this Philistine to fight with him: **FOR THOU ART A YOUTH**, and he a man of war from his youth.

MANY MONTHS AGO, I was returning home to Ellsworth after visiting a parishioner in a hospital in Bangor. As I travelled the 20 plus miles back, I turned my car radio on to a local Christian station to catch a few tunes. As the music played I must admit I had my mind more focused on the sickness of the man I had visited rather than on the music being played or the song being sung. However, as the song that was playing reached the end of the music a phrase broke through my spirit and invaded my soul. The words of the singer were simple: **"Deep inside the armour, the warrior is a child!"** I don't know who wrote or recorded those words, or even if that is the title of the song? For I have never heard it since, yet I have come to believe those words are a wonderful commentary on David's battle with the giant Goliath and our battle against Satan to this day. You may be just a child spiritually, you may be a coward naturally, and you maybe a codger in age, or a cripple physically, but 'deep inside the armour of God there is courage and peace and protection against all of the Goliaths of life. Each morning when you get up and put on the armour of God (Ephesians 6:10–18) you can defeat any foe. That is why each morning you must not forget to put on the whole armour of God; it is your only defense against the giants you will face. David didn't forget, so when he got to the battle of Elah unaware of what he was going to find, he was still ready to meet God's foe head on, safe inside the armour of the Living God. Paul exhorts all believers: "The night is far spend, the day is at hand: let us therefore cast off the works of darkness, and let us put on the armour of Light." (Romans 13:12) Deep inside the armour of God we are able to confront any work of darkness, or worker of darkness, even giant ones.

The spiritual armour is the Christian's uniform (II Timothy 2:3–4). As Christian warriors we need to be 'dressed for success', why? A number of years ago someone wrote a song with this thought in mind: **"deep inside the armour, the warrior is a child"**! I would like to use their concept to teach you the importance of putting on 'the whole armour of God.... that you may be able to stand against the wiles of the devil'. Through the experience of the youngest of all the 'giant-killer', you can be trained in the protection that the armour of God affords because "Deep Inside The Armour......."

1. **THE WARRIOR COULD BE A CHILD**. I Samuel 17:33. David was not a soldier but a shepherd and a shepherd-boy at that, yet on that day of battle with a giant he took on the enemy's best and beat him, not because of Saul's armour (I Samuel 17:38–39), but because of God's armour! Who needs the armour more than a 'baby' in Christ? John speaks in his First Epistle about 'little children', new believers (I John 2:12), people who have just had their sins forgiven. Is there anyone more open to a giant attack from Satan that a new believer, yet deep inside the armour he or she is just as protected as any mature saint? I was reading once about the way Japanese fighter pilots of the Second World War protected their rookie fighter pilots. They would put those young pilots in the planes of their aces (pilots with more than five victories). Enemy pilots seeing the kill markings on the side of the planes would stay away thinking an ace was behind the stick. Little did they know that deep inside of the cockpit the pilot was a rookie? Deep inside the armour the giant can't tell either! Goliath seemingly had no fear of David because he only saw a child (I Samuel 17:42). What he failed to see was the amour of God around that 'youth'!

2. **THE WARRIOR COULD BE A COWARD**. Joshua 1:6, 7, 9. Why did God have to encourage Joshua three times? Because deep inside

the armour was the heart of a coward, yet Joshua went on to become one of the bravest 'giant-killer' in the Bible (Joshua 11:21–22), how? The armour of God (Joshua 24:18) gives the Christian soldier courage (II Timothy 1:7). Many a coward has become a hero simply because their enemy doesn't know they are a coward. The armour hides fear behind the 'shield of faith' (Ephesians 6:16) and blocks that fear from your enemy. Some of the greatest men and women of the Bible were afraid, but deep inside the armour of God they accomplished great feats and so can we: if we live deep inside the armour of God. As we have already discovered in our search for Satan's Super Soldiers, one of the first aspects we must conquer before we take on a giant is fear. Our fear will come under control and our confidence will soar when we step behind the armour God has provided for us.

3. **THE WARRIOR COULD BA A CODGER.** Joshua 14:10–15. A 'codger' is an old man. Remember, Caleb was 85 when he started his assault on the giants of Hebron and the surrounding towns occupied by 'giants'. Some would say he was too old to take on such a task, yet he proved despite his age that he was more than up for the task. One of the greatest deceptions of the Devil is to convince people that they are too old to sign up for the Lord's Army, or too old to re-sign with the Lord's warriors, so they resign to an old folks complex in Florida wasting what might be their most productive years. Yes, deep inside the armour the warriors maybe a senior citizen, an elderly saint, an old soldier, but let us never forget this admonition from the pen of Paul: "For which cause we faint not; but though our outward man perish, yet the inward man is renewed day by day." (II Corinthians 4:16) We can be renewed, revived, and refreshed by resting 'deep inside the armour', so it is time we sign up, re-up and take on the 'giants' of old age!

4. **THE WARRIOR COULD BE A CRIPPLE.** II Samuel 21:15–17. David was crippled by age the final time he faced his last giant (more in another chapter) in the concluding battle of his illustrious career, yet he prevailed, he survived, why? In the Battle of Gob, David trusted in the God he learned to trust when he was a lad. As the blows of Goliath's brother knocked him to the ground, David's only defense until a fellow soldier came to help him was the eternal shield of the Almighty, Living God. Faith in God will strengthen your resolve and will overcome any weaknesses and shortcomings you might have. It is simply amazing what the armour of God will help you overcome: age,

handicaps, fear, and youth. It's time we duck behind the armour and see what God can do for us in the fight.

I know not what your shortcoming is in the battle for life, but I do know we all have 'a thorn in the flesh' whether youthfulness, cowardliness, a weakness, or just plain oldness! This I have learned from the numerous stories of ordinary men going up against 'giants', is what God can do through those men despite their shortcomings. This might just be one of the best lessons I have learned in this study of Satan's Super Soldiers, the Devil's warriors can't recognize who is really behind the armor of God, even when they recognize the child!

36

ULTIMATELY
THE BATTLE IS THE LORD'S

I Samuel 17:47-And all this assembly shall know that the Lord saveth not with sword and spear: for **THE BATTLE IS THE LORD'S,** and he will give you into our hands.

EVER SINCE I FIRST read about the historic account of the confrontation between the infamous German battleship Bismarck and the famous British battle cruiser Hood in the Denmark Straits during the Second World War, I have been fascinated with battles, all battles, land battles, sea battles, and battles in the skies. The titanic struggles between nations or navies, armies or armadas has ever since peaked my interest. Whether the Battle of Gettysburg during the great American Civil War, or the battle of Waterloo, when one of the world's greatest generals, Napoleon, meet his "waterloo"; battles have been such a part of World History one can't study history without studying 'battles', and as General Sir John Hackett has written: "Warfare is one of the oldest occupations known to man. It is as ancient and enduing as song and measurement and is likely to persist as long as man remains what he is: contentious, tribal, acquisitive, and prone to impose solutions by force." And as I have discovered in this study of Satan's Super Soldiers, even the Bible is a book of battles. (I have compiled a book I call Bible Battles-60 famous and not so famous actual military battles recorded in the Word of God. Over 400 pages long it is my largest book project to date!)!

During my reading of the Bible I have discovered that there are some books the Bible mentions that we no longer have a copy of, like: "Wherefore it is said in **the book of the wars of the Lord**......" (Numbers 21:14) Wouldn't I love a copy of that book! In reading the commentaries on this most suggest that at one time there was a book that had recorded "Bible Battles". There are some who suggest it was written by a man by the name of Jasher, and this was the book Moses was referring too. David in his lamentations for his best friend Jonathon's death at the Battle of Gilboa writes: ".....teach the children of Judah the use of the bow, behold it is written in **_the book Jasher_**." (II Samuel 1:18) When Joshua was recording the unusual events associated with the battle of Gideon, one of the proofs he used to verify the facts was: "Is not this written in **_the book Jasher_**?" (Joshua 10:13) I have become persuaded that the Book of Jasher was a compiling of the notable battles in the history of the children of Israel, so the Battles of the Lord! Our problem today is the fact that this book never survived the Old Testament, but another book did and does to this day: the Bible! This has been my goal in this book to re-record the battles of the Lord with Satan's Super Soldiers; to glean from the pages of God's war book the significant battles of Biblical history fought against the 'giants'. This has not been a chronological or historical exercise only but a spiritual quest into the lessons we can learn from these titan and titanic struggles between God's men and Satan's 'giants'. Perhaps, at the heart of the lessons we have learned is this shout of a shepherd boy at the Battle of Elah when he proclaimed: **"The Battle is the Lord's"** (I Samuel 17:47)!

I have come to an understanding of all the precepts that we have uncovered about 'giants', this might be the greatest, and as we have apply this concept in past battles with 'giants', we will apply to the many battles left to be uncovered! David certainly wanted Goliath to know this principle before he killed him, and from that ancient battlefield of old this saying has rung truth throughout the ages on all battlefields and in all battles. It is typical of us to lose sight of this byword as we struggle many times against staggering odds in our own corner of the battlefield of life; thinking the battle is ours and ours alone, and the outcome of the battle is ours and ours alone. It is at time like this we need to learn that **'to do nothing is better than to do something'**! We live in a world in which the philosophy is exactly the opposite-to do something is better than to do nothing! King Jehoshaphat of Judah had to learn this lesson at the Battle of Jerval. It was through the prophet Jahaziel God told Jehoshaphat this: "Thus saith the Lord unto you, be not afraid, nor dismayed by reason of this great multitude; ***for the battle is not yours, but God's***. Tomorrow, go ye down against them.....ye shall not need to fight in this battle, set yourself, stand still, and see the salvation of the Lord...." (II Chronicles 20:14–17) Moses and Israel also had to learn this lesson at the battle of the Red Sea when Jehovah told them: "Fear ye not, stand still, and see the salvation of the Lord.....***The Lord shall fight for you***, and ye shall hold your peace." (Exodus 14:13–14) David had learned his Sunday school lessons well for when he stepped out on the battlefield against Goliath he knew that whether he fought or not the fight was really God's. Have we learned this lesson yet?

The Sunday School Times once printed this inspiring truth: **"When God alone can win the victory, faith lets God do it all. It is better to trust than try?"** Again totally contrary to the philosophy of the world that is all about 'trying'! How many times have you been caught fighting God's battles? It is as if we think our God is too small, too weak to fight his own battles! I am having a hard time understanding the 'apologists' in the Church today. The modern Church seems to be all about defense, and I am not saying we shouldn't (Jude 3), but a good offense is our best defense. David didn't stand waiting for Goliath to attack him, but he attacked Goliath and God did the fighting (I Samuel 17:48)! Whether hourly, daily, weekly, or yearly, battles rage in and around us constantly. Some are lifelong in duration, but whose battles are they really? H. E. Jessop once wrote a poem with this idea in mine: "The battle is not yours, but God's, therefore why fight? True faith will cease from struggling and rest upon His might: each conflict into which you come, was won on Calvary, tis ours to claim what Christ has done, and hold the victory!" So many are prone to action, I know I am, to do something when in reality God would have us spectators, not soldiers. The great Church father Saint Jerome once said: **"The most difficult precept of action sinks into nothingness, when compared with God's command of inaction!"** Is not that what God said to Jehoshaphat and Moses and I believe to David as well despite it not being recorded in the story of I Samuel 17!

So if, **"the battle is the Lord's"** then the responsibility for strategy, supply, and success are His as well! As David approached Goliath he was as the stone in his sling, just an instrument in the hand of the Lord because it wasn't David's battle but God's! I like what the great English monarch, Queen Elizabeth I, once said: "We are not interested in the possibilities of defeat. It does not exist!" David ran toward Goliath and the army of the

Philistines with only one thought: "the battle is the Lord's", and my Lord has never been defeated, He has never lost! We too can go into the Lord's battles in our life with the same confidence because the Apostle Paul has taught us: "Now thanks be unto God which ALWAYS causeth us to triumph in Christ…." (II Corinthians 2:14) and "Thanks be to God which giveth us the victory through our Lord Jesus….." (I Corinthians 15:57)

My prayer and my desire is that the account of these defeats of Satan's Super Soldiers will settle your troubled spirit in the up and coming battles of your life; and that you will be able to say with confidence as each begins: **"I will not fear the battle, if Thou art on my side!"** Whether an actual battle, or a spiritual battle, I have come to believe in David's philosophy demonstrated at the Battle of Elah. David might never have thought just how he might kill Goliath, but he knew that the battle was ultimately in God's hands!

37

LESSONS FROM DAVID'S VICTORY OVER GOLIATH

I Samuel 17:51-Therefore **DAVID** ran, and stood upon **THE PHILISTINE,** and took his sword, and drew it out of the sheath thereof, and slew him, and cut off his head therewith. And when the Philistines saw their champion was dead, they fled.

WE WILL END OUR extensive look at the defeat of Goliath with these final observations and lessons we can learn when fighting our 'giants'!

The first lesson I feel we need to highlight in fighting 'giants' is the danger of *'wearing Saul's armour'* (I Samuel 17:38). How was it that David sought the Lord's protection over the king's protection? I like Oswald Chambers on this lesson: "If your religious injures your intelligence, it is bad; if it injures your character, it is vicious; if it injures your conscience, it is criminal. Therefore don't try and wear Saul's armour. It is pathetic to see us when we are about a month old in grace trying to wear the terrific amour of a mature saint; we go about clanking great sentiments on profound themes while our practical life laughs at us. If we obey God, He will introduce us by the current events and by our obedience into the place where these truths become real to us, and we begin to 'grow up into Him in all things'. **Anything that releases us from personal accountability to Jesus Christ is corrupt**." This explanation reminds me of what Paul warned the early Christians when it came in choosing a pastor: "Not a novice, lest being lifted up with pride he fall into the condemnation of the devil. More-over he must have a good report of them which are without; lest he fall into the reproach and the snare of the devil." (I Timothy 3:6–7) David escaped all three: 'the condemnation of the devil', 'the reproach of the devil', and 'the snare of the devil' when he refused Saul's amour for his up and coming battle with Goliath. So must we not be tricked by thinking man's protection is better than God's protection in the battles of life!

The second lesson we need to underline in fighting 'giants' is the danger of *'carrying Saul's sword'* (I Samuel 17:39). How was it that David put more trust in his sling than in Saul's sword? I like Charles Spurgeon on this lesson: "It is a grand thing to have no sword in the hand of David, and yet for David to know that his God will overthrow a whole army of aliens (Hebrews 11:34). If we are indeed contending for the truth and righteous-ness, let us not tarry till we have talent, or wealth, or any other form of visible power at our disposal; but with such stones as we find in the brook, and with our own usual sling, let us run to meet the enemy. If it were our own battle, we might not be confident; but if we are standing up for Jesus, and warring in His strength alone, who can withstand us? (Romans 8:31) Without a trace of hesitancy, let us face the Philistines; for the Lord of Host is with us, and who can be against us?" Manmade swords are no match for a God-made sword (Ephesians 6:17). A verse we have mentioned numer-ous times in this search for Satan's Super Soldiers is Zechariah 4:6: "....*Not by might, nor by power, but by my Spirit,* saith the Lord of Hosts." Besides, according to our key verse printed above, there was a sword already at the battlefront that David could use to kill the giant!

The third lesson we need to understand in fighting 'giants' is the danger of *'believing Saul's argument'* (I Samuel 17:33). How was it that David didn't believe the logical, rational, and reasonable argument of King Saul? I like Mrs. Charles Cowman on this lesson: "It is a source of inspiration and strength to come in touch with the youthful David, trusting God. Through faith in God he conquered a lion and a bear, and afterward overthrew the mighty Goliath. When that lion came to despoil that flock, it came as a wonderful opportunity to David. If he had failed or faltered he would have missed God's opportunity for him and probably would never have come to be God's chosen king of Israel. One would not think that a lion was a spe-cial blessing from God; God's opportunity in disguise. Every difficulty that presents itself to us, if we receive it in the right way, is God's opportunity. May God open our eyes to see Him, whether in temptations, trials, dangers, or misfortunes?" We must be watchful for human understanding verses simple trusting God. If the battle is the Lord's, whether lion, or bear, or giant, then the opportunity exists for us to grow in our trust and confidence in the Almighty; granted, Saul's argument seemed to all, but David, the best advice with the situation at hand and the circumstance on the battlefield, but David looked beyond and so must we if we are to fight God's way verses man's way (Isaiah 55:8–9)!

The last lesson I see we must learn in fighting 'giants' is the danger of *'imitating Saul's fear'* (I Samuel 17:11). How was it that David wasn't as impressed with Goliath as Saul and his soldiers were? I like F. B. Meyer on this lesson: "The armies of the living-God-I Samuel 17:26, 36; this made all the difference between David and the rest of the camp. To Saul and his soldiers God was an absentee: a name, but little else. They believed that He had done great things for His people in the past and that at some future time, in the days of the Messiah, He might be expected to do great things again; but no one thought of Him as present. Keenly sensitive to the defiance of the Philistines, and grieved by the apathy of his people, David, on the other hand, felt that God was alive. He had lived alone with Him in the solitude of the hills, till God had become one of the greatest and most real facts of his young existence; and as the lad went to and fro among the armed warriors, he was sublimely conscious of the presence of the Living God amid the clang of the camp. This is what we need. To live so much with God, that when we come amongst men, whether in the bazaars of India or the market-place of an English town, we may be more aware of His overshadowing presence than of the presence or absence of any one. Lo, God is here! This place is hallowed ground! We can face the mightiest foe in His name. If our faith can but make Him a passage, along which He shall come, there is no Goliath He will not quell; no question He will not answer; no need He will not meet!" Fear more often than not causes more fear. That was the trauma in Saul's camp when David arrived, yet David didn't fall victim to that fear, why? I believe again as we have seen often in these giant stories was the presence of faith. Saul had no faith in his soldiers, or himself, but David had faith in his God and as a result in himself. Too many of us are listening to our fears and imitating those around us instead of believing in God and watching for Him at the battlefront. It is time to set our focus on the right examples around us not men like Saul that have no spiritual insight, but to men, even young men, who wear God's armour, who carry God's sword, who believe God's argument, and who imitate God's men!

Postscript: before I leave this verse I want to highlight and underline another characteristic of Satan and his Super Soldiers. We often overlook the agreement that Goliath was offering to the Israelites (I Samuel 17:9): if he won then Israel would be subservient to Philistia, but if the Israelite won the Philistines would be subservient to the Israelites. Note the final two words of our key verse printed above: *'they fled'*! Remember this, Satan is a liar (John 8:44) and he will never keep any deal he makes and neither will any of his servants, giants or others. No deal will be upheld by him or them!

38

DAVID'S LITTLE KNOWN BATTLES WITH GIANTS

II Samuel 5:18, 22-The Philistines also came and spread themselves in the valley of Rephaim (**GIANTS**).......And the Philistines came up yet again, and spread themselves in the valley of Rephaim (**GIANTS**).

IF THERE IS ONE area in Christian soldiering against giants that is lacking today in the average spiritual warrior it is the characteristic of '*quickness*'! What I mean by the use of the word '*quickness*' is the desire to respond immediately to the Lord's instructions and commandments at a time of crisis. Remember when the Lord was looking for disciples and he found Peter and Andrew that he said: "Follow me, and I will make you fishers of men." (Matthew 4:19) Did they ponder the request? Did they tell Jesus they would give him their answer in a week? Did they drag their feet at His command? No! "And they **straightway** left their nets, and followed him!" (Matthew 4:20) James and John responded in a similar fashion (Matthew 4:22). Where is straightwayness and immediateness in the church of God today? Could this be one of the reasons the Church is being defeated on the battle front, on so many battlefields? Have we been to slow in responding to the Lord's commands and the threats of our enemies? Timing is everything on the battlefield, the difference between victory and defeat many times. Being too slow can change the outcome of most battles, especially with giants, and I see this clearly in David's early battles after he became king when his archenemy the Philistines were determined to defeat David, and if there were giants at the Battle of Elah surely there were giants at the First and Second Battle of Rephaim (the battles in the valley of giants)?

Despite the fact that no specific giant is mentioned in II Samuel 5, we know from our comparison of I Samuel 17 and II Samuel 21 that there was more than one giant in the Philistine ranks from the reign of King Saul to the rule of King David. It is my belief that every time David took the field of battle against Philistia he and his men faced giants. I see this vital lesson played out for us in the fight that would become known as the Battles of Geba and Gazer (II Samuel 5:25). These conflicts between Israel and Philistia took place in **'the valley of the giants'**. Our Scripture above suggests that there were two separate battles here (read carefully II Samuel 5:17–25). Philistia was a thorn in the side of Israel throughout Saul's rule and continued in through David's reign. The Philistines lived on the coastal plain of the Promised Land and once David made Jerusalem his capital (II Samuel 5:6–10), the Philistines needed to weaken his kingdom and the best route to Jerusalem was up through the Valley of Rephaim. In 2010, I had a chance to visit Israel and travelled through **'the valley of giants'** a number of times seeing firsthand the strategic position, an open and direct route to Jerusalem, the heartland of Israel.

David had established his capital in the old Jebusite city after seven years in Hebron (II Samuel 5:5), and these early invasions by the Philistine army was intended to send a message to the young king and the newly united nation. Upon hearing of the advance of the Philistine army David immediately enquired of the Lord what to do (II Samuel 5:19), and through his immediate implementation of the Lord's strategy David was able to win a great victory. What I find exciting about David is the fact that he didn't make the same mistake that Joshua made after this victory over Jericho (Joshua 7). Just because the situation and circumstance seems the same, David didn't take for granted that the next battle would need the same strategy as Joshua did at Ai. It was a good thing David sought the Lord for a second time because it says: "And when David enquired of the Lord, he said, Thou shalt not go up; but fetch a compass behind them, and come upon them over against the mulberry trees." (II Samuel 5:23) There seems to be a popular misconception in Christian circles that our enemies don't learn from their defeats (that seems to be more our problem). God knew the Philistines were smart warriors. No doubt they were ready for David's attack tactics after the first Battle of Rephaim. Most successful commanders never use the same strategy twice because after a stunning defeat, like the Philistines suffered at the Battle of Baalperazim (II Samuel 5:20), the official title of this battle, they would change their tactics for the next battle, as do Satan's Super Soldiers!

I like what Charles Haddon Spurgeon says about this concept in his great devotional Book 'Morning and Evening", and I quote: "When David made this enquiry he had last fought the Philistines, and gained a signal victory. The Philistines came up in great hosts, but, by the help of God, David had easily put them to flight. Note, however, that when they came the second time, David did not go up to fight them without enquiring of the Lord. Once he had been victorious, and he might have said, as many have in other cases, 'I shall be victorious again; I may rest quite sure that if I have conquered once I shall triumph again. Wherefore should I tarry to seek at the Lord's hands?' Not so, David. He had gained one battle by the strength of the Lord; he would not venture upon another until he had ensured the same. He enquired, 'Shall I go up against them?' He waited until God's sign was given. Learn from David to take no step without God. Christian, if thou wouldn't know the path of duty, takes God for thy compass; if thou wouldst steer thy ship through the dark billows, put the tiller into the hands of the Almighty. Many a rock might be escaped, if we would let our Father take the helm; many a shoal or quicksand we might well avoid, if we would leave to His sovereign will to choose and to command. The Puritan said, 'As sure as ever a Christian carves for himself, he'll cut his own fingers;' this is a great truth. Said another old divine, 'He that goes before the cloud of God's providence goes on a fool's errand;' and so he does. We must mark God's providence, we'll be very glad to run back again. 'I will instruct thee and teach thee in the way thou shalt go' (Proverbs 3:5) is God's promise to His people. Let us, then, take all our perplexities to Him, and say, 'Lord, what wilt thou have me to do?' (Acts 9:6) Leave not thy chamber this morning without enquiring of the Lord." Could I add, because a giant might be waiting for you down the road!

David won in my opinion the Battle of Geba because he enquired of the Lord, acted promptly on God's instructions, and straightway gained a great victory. God's timing is perfect, and so was David's because he listened to the Lord. David's second battle in the valley of Rephaim was a flanking movement behind the advancing Philistine army and when God's wind signaled the attack (II Samuel 5:24) David struck. When God signals us to action, so should be our response. To strike when the iron is hot is an old saying but a true one. To attack when the tide has turned is also a great application to this precept, and to advance when the time is right takes great sensitivity on our behalf to the leading of the Lord. It also takes a great *'quickness'*. Do you have it; do you have the will to ask God and then wait on God. Joshua learned this lesson the hard way at the Battle of Ai (Joshua 8:19), but David learned it the easy way, how? We often forget that the precept that David was 'a man after God's own heart' (Acts 13:22) can be applied to every aspect of David's life, including his military life. Why hasn't the Church of God; why hasn't most Christians learned this principle? Before we finish, we will note that each giant was defeated in turn by a giant-killer who listened and changing quickly their strategy!

39

DAVID'S MIGHTY MEN IN GIANT COUNTRY

II Samuel 23:13-And three of the thirty chief went down, and came to David in the harvest time unto the cave Adullam: and the troop of the Philistines pitched in the valley of Rephaim (**GIANTS**).

THE BATTLE OF BETHLEHEM took place when David was a fugitive in the wilderness just south of his hometown trying to stay one step ahead of a vengeful King Saul who wanted to kill him because he felt threatened by David popularity (I Samuel 18). David's first official headquarters was located in a cave called Adullam. I Samuel 22:1–2 tell us about David's first hideout, an area he would have known because of grazing his father's sheep. I believe David also wrote Psalm 142 in this cave! Located within a few miles of Bethlehem, I imagine David explored the cave as a shepherd, but found it a strategic fortress as a soldier. The story we are telling in this devotional on Satan's Super Soldiers say it was 'harvest time', a hot period in southern Judah. David got thirsty and began to desire a drink of the cool water that came from a well near the gate into Bethlehem. It is my opinion that David was thinking out-loud ("And David longed, and said, Oh that one would give me drink of the water of the well of Bethlehem, which is by the gate."-II Samuel 23:15) when three (Adino, Eleazar, and Shammah-II Samuel 23:8–12) of his men overheard him. I don't believe David would have ever ordered his mighty men to venture into Bethlehem for just some water when we read: "And David was then in an hold, and the garrison of the Philistines was then in Bethlehem." (II Samuel 23:14) Bethlehem was a dangerous place, and the land between Adullam and Bethlehem was even more dangerous because the Philistines were encamped in great numbers throughout 'the Valley of Rephaim (giants)' (II Samuel 23:13). To get into Bethlehem David's soldiers would have to fight a Philistine army which, as we have seen, included 'giants!

Whether David had been thinking out loud, or had casually mentioned the desire for a drink of water from Bethlehem's well, the news spread like wildfire around the cave. The resulting action by three of David's 'mighty men' proves in my mind once and for all of the enthusiastic devotion of David's soldiers to their captain (I Samuel 22: 2). They were willing to put their lives on the line for this young shepherd, and were ready at the drop of a hat to fulfill his smallest wish even at the risk of their own lives. If such men existed in the band that joined David in Adullam, shouldn't such men exist in the disciple band? I believe we can find such 'mighty men' in the first century followers of Jesus, for men like Peter, James, and John did such things for Christ, but what about now. Paul taught us: "Thou therefore, endure hardness as a good soldier of Jesus Christ....that he might please him who hath chosen him to be a soldier." (II Timothy 2:3–4) Christ's wish ought to be our command; not that He always commands as to do or go, but we ought to do or go because of our great love and affection for Him; our loyalty and devotion for Him even in the face of an alien army and a troop of giants, according to His instructions!

As you read the story recorded in II Samuel 23:13–17, remember, these three warriors had to leave their 'stronghold' (II Samuel 23:14 NIV) exposing themselves to their enemy through the Valley of Rephaim, which means 'valley of the giants' and remember the Philistines not only were in control of this valley named after the giants, but there was still giants in their army at this time (II Samuel 21:15–19)! These men would have had to defend themselves as they got the water out of the well which was near the city gate. Usually the gate of a city is the weakest part of the defenses of a city, so more defenders were stationed there. Even if they got to the city without rousing suspicion, they would have altered the garrison by the time they got the water resulting in their needing to fight their way back to Adullam. The Old King James Version of the Bible uses the words "brake through" (II Samuel 23:16), so I don't believe they snuck in and out, stealth was not used. I believe they fought their way there, fought there, and fought their way back!

"And brought it (the water) to David." (II Samuel 23:16) The trio won the Battle of Bethlehem or the Battle for a Cup of Water; how many they killed to accomplish this mission I know not, but three wonderful qualities between these three had to be present if they accomplished their mission. **First, I recognize loyalty.** An old church hymn says: "A call for loyal soldiers comes to one and all." In The Preacher's Magazine there was once recorded this saying: "God measures loyalty to Himself, not by expressions of feeling, but by service!" When it comes to loyalty, actions do speak louder than words. **Second, I recognize charity.** That old church hymn goes on to say: "He calls us for he loves us." John writes: "We love Him because He first loved us." (I John 4:19) Why did David's men love him so they were willing to sacrifice themselves for him? I believe it was because he had first grown to love them for their willingness to join him at his lowest time (I Samuel 22:1–2). **Lastly, I recognize unity.** There must have been a tremendous oneness among the three as they battled their way to and through Bethlehem. I believe they were as Paul exhorted the Church at Philippi to be: "...likeminded, having the same love, being of one accord, of one mind." (Philippians 2:2) If only the soldiers of Jesus Christ were so united; there wouldn't be a fort of evil, a force of wickedness, or a foe of Satan that could resist their onslaught. The trouble today is you can't find three Christians that can agree on much. David would eventually write in one of his psalms, perhaps, thinking of these three special soldiers: "Behold, how good and how pleasant it is for brethren to dwell together in unity." (Psalm 133:1) I know this characteristic is not found mentioned in Paul's 'armor of God' (Ephesians 6:10–18), but if not found in the heart of the Soldier of Christ, the spiritual armour will be a hollow fortress against 'giants'!

W. S. Brown ends his classic warrior's hymn (As a Volunteer), with these words: "And when the war is over and the victory is won, when the true and faithful gather one by one. He will crown with glory all who there appear, will you be enlisted as a volunteer?" I feel there will be a special reward waiting to honor volunteers, like the three mighty men of David that risked life and limb for some water! Recruits and draftees will receive their reward, but I believe volunteers will receive a greater reward. Isaiah was one of those volunteers (Isaiah 6:8), are you? Few volunteer to go up against 'giants', remember, Caleb was one (Joshua 14), and even if the three didn't face a giant, they were going into giant country and they knew it, yet they went, and even when David poured the water on the ground as a sacrifice to God (II Samuel 23:17) I believe they would have done it again if David would have asked. How we need to revive the spirit of volunteerism again in the Army of Christ! We have too many waiting for instruction instead of acting upon what we already know the Lord desires of us. We have too many waiting to be drafted when Christ's command to 'go' (Matthew 28:19) has already been delivered. In my reading of the biographies of the great missionaries of the 19th century (Hudson Taylor, C. T. Studd, David Livingstone) I have concluded they were all volunteers. Men and women who are willing to go into giant county for 'a cup of cold water' (Matthew 10:42) will receive their reward at the hand of their Captain!

40

THE BATTLES OF GOB
THE GIANTS LAST STAND

II Samuel 21:18-And it came to pass after this, that there was again a battle with the Philistines at Gob: then Sibbechai the Hushathite slew Saph, which was of the sons of the **GIANT**.

IT WILL TAKE US a few articles to describe and define 'the giant's last stand', but as for the Word of God this is the last chapter in the history of Satan's Super Soldiers. In a place called "Gob", these gigantic, evil warriors meet their match in a series of titanic struggles against David and his mighty men. These are also the last of the 'giant-killers' recorded in the Bible, and their defeat of the last remaining 'giants' found in the army of Philistia.

"Gob" means: a pit or a hollow. When you read II Samuel 21:15-22, the author indicates that three separate battles took place at Gob, with the final battle recorded against the giants taking place in their stronghold of Gath. In the I Chronicles 20:4 account of the first battle, Gath seems to be the site of the battle, so my conclusion is that "Gob" was a place near the Philistine city-state of Gath, a famous pit, or a geographical hollow? I have also come to the conclusion in my study of David's wars that this series of battles took place near the end of David's reign when Philistia was his only remaining, unconquered foe. Early in his kingship the Philistines were taking the fight to him (II Samuel 5:17-25), but now David and his men 'went down' (II Samuel 21:15), down from Jerusalem to attack the Philistines in

Philistia. As with the series of battles in the valley of the giants (Rephaim), so now a series of battle at "Gob"! "Gob" suggests a common location where both the men of David and the giants of Gath (II Samuel 21:22) met in mortal combat. David records not only the battles, but the heroes of each of the battles.

Rare is the place that numerous battles have been fought, but history does contain some examples. On the border between Italy and Yugoslavia (Serbia today), near the Isonzo River is a place called 'Caporetto'. Between October 17 and November 7, 1917, during World War One, a lengthy battle was fought there between the forces of a combined Austria and German army and the Italian army. It has been recorded in the journals of military history as the 12th Battle of Isonzo; that through history eleven others military battles have been fought over that same site. Also during the First World War there were at least three separate battles fought in a place called Ypres, in Flanders: in 1914, 1915, and 1917. Located 130 miles north-west of Constantinople (Istanbul today) is the Adrianople region. This area and town commanded the approaches to the famous city and the Bosporus waterway. No fewer than seven important battles were fought there: the first in July 323 and the last in February and March 1913. Repeated battles in the same location suggests importance for both the combatants and the strategic location and for some reason the Philistines and the Israelites were draw to "Gob" to battle. The repeated battles also suggests that neither side was able to totally control the area, so the battles were renewed when either side felt strong enough to attack again. What is unique about these battles is that a giant was the champion for Philistia just like the Battle of Elah where David first won his fame battling Goliath. It is time for others within David's military elite to step up and fight a giant and win their fame, just like their commander!

These battles for "Gob" seem to have taken place in the latter years of David's rule. Despite the fact the Philistines couldn't threaten Israel as they had in the days of King Saul and the early day of King David, as long as they had a giant in their ranks they believed they could win any battle. Such is the case with the last giant: Satan. Satan goes into each battle with the belief that he can win, against us or God Himself. Despite the continual defeats, and to this point in our study of Satan's Super Soldiers, there has not been a victory except for the psychological victory they won at Kadash. We will witness four more super soldiers as they challenge God's army in hand-to-hand combat, but one by one they too will go down in defeat at the hands of David's mighty men. Over the next ten chapters we will study the super soldier and the giant-killer, but before we name names and fight the fights I feel it is important for us to consider three broad principles when fighting giants in their last stronghold!

First, it is a foolish thing to put our faith in human strength, size, and success. Even 'giant-killers' get old. Read carefully II Samuel 21:15–17, and note that David was closer in dying at the hands of the giant Ishbibenob than he was at the hands of the giant Goliath. Satan has time for us to age, to grow weary, to weaken. The wonderful truth about this story is that Divine assistance is always available to the soldier of God no matter his or her age, or their strength. In my study of the 'giants', not once does even the Devil come to the aid of his warrior, but God was always there either Himself or through a fellow-soldier! Only God helps, Satan can only hinder (I Thessalonians 2:18)! From the first giant-killer to the last giant-killer, God's men have been ordinary men, no stronger or more skilled than any ordinary man, but each of them left their field of battle as a victor instead of a victim and I believe so can we (James 4:7)!

Second, it is a common thing to see our foe slain. Ezekiel put it this way: "And they shall not lie with the mighty that are fallen of the uncircumcised, which are gone down to hell with their weapons of war: and they have laid their swords under their heads, but their iniquities shall be upon their bones, though they were the terror of the mighty in the land of the living." (Ezekiel 32:27) The more I read that verse and ponder that scripture I am convinced that Ezekiel was writing about the death of 'giants': an epitaph of giants if you will! Did not David call the giant Goliath an 'uncircumcised Philistine' (I Samuel 17:26)? Was there one successful weapon of war used by the 'giants' (Isaiah 54:17)? Did not all the giants fall by their own swords (I Samuel 17:51)? Were they not a terror of the world (Numbers 13:33) while they lived? But are they not all fallen? Such was the fate of Satan's Super Soldiers!

Third, it is a common thing to believe that our most powerful enemies are often reserved for our last conflicts. It has been my belief (more later) that there were five 'giants' of Gath in total, but only one fought with David early in his life (Goliath). Four more were waiting their time to attack David in the last mile of the way. David began his military fame by killing one giant, but he ended his military career by killing four! Let us never forget this teaching of the Apostle Paul: "The last enemy that shall be destroyed is death!" (I Corinthians 15:26) Is not death one of the sons of Satan? A true son of Anak, Rephaim, the giant of Gath (II Samuel 21:22). The Bible tells us that most of us will have to face him in the end (Hebrews 9:27), but we have someone that has already slain this giant (Hebrews 2:10–15), our Captain, the Lord Jesus Christ. Jesus took on this giant, not at "Gob" but at Golgotha. It was there death meet its match, and though we might have to deal with the sting of death (I Corinthians 15:55), we will never have to deal with death itself. Oh, the grave might gain a victory (I Corinthians 15:55), but the war has been won (II Corinthians 2:14-I Corinthians 15:57). We all might have to go and fight a giant at "Gob", but we will never have to go to Golgotha. Our giant-killer took care of that!

41

ISHBIBENOB
THE FAINTING GIANT

II Samuel 21:16-And **ISHBIBENOB**, which was of the sons of the **GIANT**, the weight of whose spear weighted three hundred shekels of brass in weight, he being girded with a new sword, thought to have slain David.

WE HAVE COME TO our 9th named giant in our ongoing search for Satan's Super Soldiers recorded in the Scriptures. We have discovered Rephaim, Og, Anak, Arba, Sheshai, Ahiman, Talmai, Goliath, and now Ishbibenob. Someone has correctly written, **"Weary in the battle, but never weary of the battle"**; another important precept to remember when you're fighting giants. The word translated *'faint'* in II Samuel 21:15 is the Hebrew word 'uph' meaning **'to be weary'**. There is no sin in getting weary in the battle, but sin can be the result if you get weary of the battle. David can be our example of both concepts. In II Samuel 11, David's gets weary of the battle and what follows is the darkest period in David's amazing life; for the adultery with Bathsheba and the murder of Uriah were transgression that would affect David and his family for the rest of his life. Both sins were in direct result of David's getting weary of the battle because it says clearly it was a **"time when kings go forth to battle"** (II Samuel 11:1). However, David learned this lesson and never again got weary of the battle, preferring to get weary in the battle instead. Such is the background of the First Battle of Gob, in which David almost meets his match in a giant named

Ishbibenob. "Once again there was battle between the Philistines and Israel. David went down with his men to fight against the Philistines, and he became exhausted." (II Samuel 21:15 NIV) Fighting giant will do that to you!

First, we must settle where this famous battle *'was fought'*? In direct context, the place of this struggle is not mentioned, but in the broader context we can conclude that it was fought at a place called Gob. We read after this account: "In the course of time, there was another battle with the Philistines at Gob," (II Samuel 21:18 NIV) and "in another battle with the Philistines at Gob." (II Samuel 21:19 NIV) I have come to the reasonable deduction that over a period of time there were three separate battle fought at this place called Gob, but it was at the First Battle of Gob that David almost meet his Waterloo, in a giant that cause him to faint, but in the end it would be the giant that fainted!

Second, let us notice why David *'waxed faint'*? The placement of this story in the Life of David from the Scriptures indicates that David was nearing the end of his reign as king of Israel. Some suggest that David was well into his 60s (David would die at 70- II Samuel 5:4) at the time of this battle. Also the concern of the people about David being in battle would also give this indication of old age (II Samuel 21:17). Matthew Henry writes this: "We have here the story of some conflicts with the Philistines, which happened, as it should seem, in the latter end of David's reign." Though David and his army had subdued Philistia, they had never conquered Philistia and as long as there was a giant in the ranks of the Philistines they were ready to take on David and his 'mighty men'. David of course was no stranger to the giants of Philistia's army because he began his military career by singlehandedly killing the great giant Goliath when he was just a boy (I Samuel 17:42). Yet in the First Battle of Gob David grew weary. Time had seemingly eroded his power and years of fighting had taken its toll and on this day of battle David got fatigued. A tiredness overcame David and for the first time he didn't have the strength to finish the fight. Age had cut his stamina, and time has sapped his strength. David perhaps thought he could 'fight the good fight', but shortly into the battle David realized his body couldn't keep up with the rest of his soldiers. The mind was indeed willing, but the flesh was weak. In David's heart, he was still brave and courageous, but his arms and his legs were beginning to fail him. Only those who have lived through the stages of life recognize what David was experiencing at the Battle of Gob. As I write this devotional I am David age, and I am being reminded every day that the "outward man is perishing". That is why I am encouraged and comforted by this precept from the pen of Paul: "For which cause we faint not, but though our outward man perish, yet the inward man is renewed day by day." (II Corinthians 4:16) So as with David, our bodily salvation must come from a source other than our own strength! (Philippians 4:13)

Third, let us notice our *'willy foe'?* From reading through the rest of the context of II Samuel 21, we know that Ishbibenob was one of Goliath's younger brothers (II Samuel 21:19, 22). Perhaps this is the reason Ishbibenob sought to kill David, to avenge the death of his brother at the hands of David, and the humiliation of his family by David (giants don't expect to lose, especially against boys). For whatever reason, Ishbibenob soon became aware of David's weariness. The Philistine champion noticed that David was fainting. Josephus, the famous Jewish historian, recorded the circumstances of this encounter this way: "A little afterward the king made war against the Philistines; and he joined battle with them, and put them to flight, he was left alone, as he was in pursuit of them; when he was quite tired down, he was seen by one of the enemy, whose name was Achmon, the son of Araph; he was one of the sons of the giant. He had a spear, the handle of which weighted 300 shekels, and a breastplate of chain work, and a sword. He turned back, and ran violently to slay their enemy's king, for he was quite tired with labor." Whether or not this is how it exactly happened, it does give an idea of how it could have happened. Our enemy is always alert to our weaknesses and our weariness. Satan is always seeking an advantage over us, and he knows that one of the best times to attack is when we are physically weak and weary, feeble and fainting. Ishbibenob perceived that David was vulnerable; that David was at a disadvantage, so he picked that time to strike, but Ishbibenob forgot: *"the battle is the Lord's"* (I Samuel 17:47)! David had done what he could up to this point; he had resisted the enemy and apparently the enemy had fled (James 4:7), but as we have learned through this trace of Satan's Super Soldiers, they only flee for a season (Luke 4:13); that they will come back especially when our weariness and limitations show themselves. Ishbibenob returned to the fight with a fury and a renewed hoped he *"thought to have slain David."* (II Samuel 21:16) Ishbibenob imagined it would be an easy fight, a simple kill because the archenemy of Philistia was tired. (David might have been tired but his God wasn't!) Our foes often are very strong, very subtle, and very successful when we are fainting, but even when we are at our worst and they are at their best we have a promise of protection from our God even when our enemy has 'a new sword'! How often have we seen this concept in these

(Isaiah 54:17) I am convinced that Ishbibenob had the new weapon created for the one purpose: to kill David with it. And that time had come!
Ishbibenob had David at his mercy. David was down and Ishbibenob was
ready to give 'the coupe la grace', the final and fatal blow, but in the wings,
off stage was a champion to save God's champion. Let us never forget this
promise: "And let us not be weary in well doing, for in due season we will
reap if we faint not." (Galatians 6:9) David's reaping in training his soldiers
it about to pay off!

42

ABISHAI
THE GIANT-KILLER

II Samuel 21:17-But **ABISHAI** the son of Zeruiah succoured him, and smote **THE PHILISTINE**, and killed him.

WHEN DAVID NUMBERED HIS 'mighty men', (I Chronicles 11:10) Abishai was fifth on that impressive list of warriors. His citation for bravery reads like this: "And Abishai the brother of Joab, he was chief of the three: for lifting up his spear against three hundred, he slew them, and had a name among the three." (I Chronicles 11:20 and II Samuel 23:18–19) What I find as interesting in this record of bravery that David leaves out the fact that Abishai singlehandedly killed a giant by the name of Ishbibenob, and in the process also saved David's life: "And Ishbibenob, which was one of the sons of the giant, the weight of whose spear weighted three hundred shekels of brass in weight, he being girded with a new sword, thought to have slain David. But Abishai, the son of Zeruiah, **succoured him** (HELPED Him), and smote the Philistine and killed him." (II Samuel 21:16–17) As amazing as that seems, David's mind drifted back to a battle in which Abishai stood in the gap and killed 300 soldiers, not one giant soldier, even if that death resulted in saving the king's life! Could that stand and memorable act of courage have taken place in a war against Edom and its most famous Battle in the Valley of Salt? For our purpose however, in our study of Satan's Super

Soldiers, we will number Abishai among the great 'giant-killers' of God's Word.

Abishai was the second of three sons born to David's sister, Zeruiah (I Chronicles 2:15–16). All of Zeruiah's boys would eventually become part of David's grand army, and all of them would excel in daring and boldness and be numbered among David's elite, his **"mighty men"**! Joab, the oldest, would become chief of staff and run David's army (I Chronicles 11:6), and Asahel, the youngest, would give his life in pursuit of the mighty warrior Abner (II Samuel 2:18–23), but Abishai was the man, the nephew, the soldier that was always there at David's side when he needed someone! In the early days when David was still being hunted down by King Saul's forces, it was Abishai who went with David one night into the camp of the enemy and pulled off a daring raid to prove to King Saul that David's was no threat to him (I Samuel 26:6–9). Later, during the rebellion of Absalom, it was Abishai who came to David's defense in David's ignoble retreat from Jerusalem (II Samuel 16:9), and it was Abishai who commanded a third of David's army in the Battle of the Ephraim Woods that won the kingdom back for David (II Samuel 18:2). He was also there at the First Battle of Gob to save David's life from a giant (II Samuel 21:15–18) which for me must have been the highlight of Abishai's military life? We want to underline in this chapter this great act of defense of his king, and for his contribution to the destruction and annihilation of one of Satan's 'giants'!

Abishai, David's watchful comrade, probably was one of David's bodyguards at the First Battle of Gob, or he was alert to the fact that David wasn't as strong as he used to be in battle and that he needed watching. As the Philistines turned tail and the army chased after them, Abishai stayed close to the king. I am reminded that like Abishai our Good Lord stays close to us in the struggle (Hebrews 13:5–6) and is ready to help when we grow weak and faint. It is important to remember that as we fight the Lord has our back and when we go down as David did that He is near like Abishai was to give us protection when the blows come from our foe. We are told by Paul (I Corinthians 15:57) to give thanks for the Lord's help, as no doubt David did for Abishai's help!

As I did in the last chapter, I will quote Josephus, for I like the way he described what Abishai did. Now we can't be sure this is exactly what happened because this is a historians account verses a Biblical accounting: "But Abishai, Joab's brother, appeared on the sudden, and protected the king with his shield, as he lay down, and slew the enemy." If Abishai wasn't afraid taking on three hundred warriors (I Chronicles 11:20), then he didn't hesitate taking on a giant! David had a cousin "that sticketh closer than a brother." (Proverbs 18:24) Matthew Henry, in his famous commentaries, makes this comment on Abishai's victory over the giant Ishbibenob: *"In spiritual conflicts, even the strong saint sometimes wax faint; then Satan attacks them furiously, but they that stand their ground, and resist him, shall be relieved, and made more than conquerors."* Let us never forget that our Good Lord will never leave us defend-less when we have grown faint in the fight, especially if we are fighting the good fight of faith!

Herb Vander Lugt, writing in an Our Daily Bread article, makes this inspiring observation on the First Battle of Gob and Abishai's valuable part in that fight: "Sometimes we win great spiritual victories or seemingly reach unattainable goals without the help of a friend or champion. This was true of David when as a shepherd lad he killed Goliath with nothing but a sling and faith in God. In later years, however, he would have been slain by a giant named Ishbibenob if his nephew Abishai had not come to his aid. Now, are we to conclude that God was with David when he met Goliath, but not when he confronted the second giant? I don't think so! The Lord simply used a different means to take care of His servant. The first time, He used David's skill with a sling; the second time, He used Abishai's strength and military prowess. Several months ago a minister came to me for counsel. He said, 'I've always been able to solve my problems by reading the Bible and praying, but somehow it's different this time.' He spoke as if seeking advice from a fellow Christian showed a lack of faith. We should never feel that way. Instead, we should thank the Lord for providing people to minister to us, than allow them to help us. A human helper may be just what you need today!" Whether a word from the Word or a warrior in a war, God's succourers are worthy of mention; remember, what Paul said of Phebe: "I commend unto you Phebe our sister, which is a servant of the church which is at Cenchrea: that ye receive her in the Lord, as becometh saints, and that ye assist her in whatsoever business she hath need of you: for she hath been a **succourer** (HELPER) of many, and myself also." (Romans 16:1–2)

I poet named Sherman once penned: "It is a joy in life to find, at every turning of the road, the strong arms of a friend so kind, to help me onward with my load." David had come to one of those corners. He was weary and faint, and he had a demonic giant breathing down his neck. It was then David's God sent Abishai, not an angel (Psalm 34:7); for Elijah it was an angel, but for David it was his boyhood companion Abishai. Christ in the Battle of

Gethsemane was sent an angel (Luke 22:43) to strengthen Him, but David just needed a fellow warrior, a younger nephew, an inferior in rank and status, but David graciously accepted Abishai's help. Are you too proud to accept help from someone younger than you? I know some saints that it is 'an angel' or no one! When weariness sets in God will send help, but are you willing to accept the help God sends? He, who will not accept help, will not be helped! Abishai not only goes down in my book as a champion, a 'giant-killer', but a helping companion. What I learned from Abishai is that 'giant-killer' aren't in it for the fame, but to simply help a fellow-soldier in the fight! So who do you need to help that is fighting a giant they can't win against except for help?

43

SAPH
THE FOLLOWING GIANT

II Samuel 21:18-And it came to pass after this, that there was again a battle with the Philistines at Gob: then Sibbechai the Hushathite slew **SAPH**, which was of the sons of the **GIANT**.

THE LAST GROUP OF Biblical 'giants' come in connection with Philistia, the land of the Philistines located on the coastal plain southwest of Jerusalem. Although the nation of Philistia had come under the dominance of David by the end of his kingship, every city-state of that hostile land hadn't been captured. There always seemed to be another battle (a following battle) with the Philistines, and as long as Philistia had a gigantic champion they would prove a dangerous adversary. No doubt each time one of these titan stepped on the field of battle they brought a resurgence of courage to the Philistine Army. Four consecutive battles are recorded in Second Samuel 21 in which a giant was involved, but as with all the other battles with giants we have traced in our study of Satan's Super Soldiers, *".....the battle was the Lord's...."* (I Samuel 17:47) and the giant was defeated.

In the Second Battle for Gob (the first battle was recorded in II Samuel 21:15–17), it was a giant named Saph that confronted David's mighty men. As with David's first battle with a Philistine giant (Goliath), Philistia believed that despite the previous defeats, Saph would be the giant that would turn the tide on a string of Israeli victories. But as we read in our key verse printed above Saph died like the giants before him: Og (Deuteronomy 3:11), Anak (Numbers 13:33), Arba (Joshua 14:15), Goliath (I Samuel 17:51), Rapha (Genesis 14:5), and Ishbibenob (II Samuel 23:17). Remember, we have come to the conclusion that there was at least two races of 'giants' in the Promised Land: Rapha (Rephaims) and Anak (Anakims). I have come to believe that Saph was from the race of Rapha, and despite his size and stature and skill he was slain by one of David's ordinary soldiers: "In the course of time, war broke out with the Philistines at Gezer (or Gob). At that time Sibbechai the Hushathite killed Sippai (or Saph), one of the descendants of the Rephaims, and the Philistines were subjugated." (I Chronicles 20:4)

Who slew the giant Saph? Does it take a titan to kill a giant? Does it take a Samson to slay one of Satan's Super Soldiers? No, it only takes a man of faith and courage to face his fears and let God win the victory. Sibbechai is not a household name even in a Bible reading house. But Sibbechai was numbered among David's 'mighty men' (I Chronicles 11:29). Perhaps, it was Sibbechai only call to fame on the battlefield, but that fight got him into David's 'hall of fame', a list of David's mightiest warriors. We know little of this famous fight, for the Second Battle of Gob gets only two verses in the Holy Canon, but it is enough to immortalize Sibbechai; we will highlight this man in our next chapter.

The Devil can put some pretty big giants on the battlefields of our lives; opponents that by size seem undefeatable, invincible, and intimidating. They loom high over us seemingly undaunted and indestructible, yet we have discovered in our research through the Bible: they are but mirages, shadows! As I finish up my study I have discovered that every giant, without exception, was eventually defeated by God's man. There is not one recorded victory by one giant in a face to face conflict, and every one that did confront a man of God went down to defeat. Granted, Satan's giants did have their victories when they used fear against their foe (Numbers 13:33), but a courageous man they couldn't win against; no matter their weaponry! I found it interesting that Samson, God's strongest man in the Bible, fought many a Philistine, but he never faced a giant, why; because **"God chose the weak things of the world to shame the strong."** (I Corinthians 1:27 NIV) That is why when it was time to face a giant God called on men like Sibbechai to do the job! What kind of glory does God get (I Corinthians 1:29) when a titan like Samson defeats a giant like Saph. I have come to see this story of Sibbechai as one of an ordinary soldier in the frontline of David's army at the Second Battle of Gob, but when the battle was over Sibbechai was added to that rare and unique Biblical class of 'giant-killer'. I feel Sibbechai went into that battle not knowing the giant he would face, as we go into our daily battles not knowing the foes we will face. Today we have 'men of renown' (Genesis 6:4) who still confront God's people. They might be the powerful politicians of our land attacking morality, or the intellectual giants of science attacking creationism! Noah faced the first giants I believe, and Jesus warned us that as his days so our days (Matthew 24:37), so giants we will face, but are we a Sibbechai?

Washington Gladden writes: "In the noble struggle for freedom and a united Italy against seemingly unconquerable foes and insuperable difficulties, Garibaldi flung forth to his dispirited forces this challenge: 'Soldiers! What I have to offer you is fatigue, danger, struggle and death; the chill of the cold night in open air, and heat under the burning sun; no lodging, no munitions, no provisions, but forced marches, dangerous watch posts, and the continual struggle with the bayonet against batteries. Those who love freedom and their country, follow me'. They answered the call. A brave man inspires others to heroism, but his own courage is not diminished when it enters into other souls; it is stimulated and invigorated. I shall go across battlefields and into twisting storms that I may have an experience of the Father's care, protection, and glorious deliverances! I am to share in the tremendous experiences of the great! I am builded not as a skiff but as an ocean liner to sail the high sea of the universe." I know not if David gave such a challenge before Gob to his warriors, but it sounds like something that would inspire a Sibbechai to battle Saph! What can I say for you to fight your giant?

Let us lay claim to the courage of this 'giant-killer', Sibbechai, and attack the titan, Saph, that stands before us. Was it the unrecognized draw of the battle order that put Sibbechai across the field from Saph, or did he like David seek Saph out? I call Saph the following giant because of Ishbibenob in the First Battle of Gob. Satan will always follow up an attack by one giant with another giant. As we have seen in our study of Satan's Super Soldiers, Satan always seems to have another giant in the wings to take on God's champion. I still believe that David chose five stones at Elah because he knew that Goliath had four brother, including Saph, but Satan only unleashes his giants one at a time (a really bad strategy). All giants are not for the same warrior, showing me this lesson: **we will all have to face our own giant!** It might be the giant called 'cancer', the giant called 'chronic illness', the giant called 'business failure', the giant called 'loss of a child', and a thousand other giants with scary names. We need to learn well before we face our giant on our battlefield of life, this instruction from Moses: "Only rebel not yet against the Lord, neither fear ye the people of the land (including giants); for they are bread for us: their defense is departed from them, and the Lord is with us, fear them not." (Numbers 14:9) I know not if Sibbechai took this into battle with him, but we should!

The following giants of our lives are just waiting a good time to attack us, so let us be fully armed, fully alert to counterattacks with the weapons the Lord has given us, for I believe that hot on your tail is one of Satan's Super Soldiers and we need to kill it!

44

SIBBECHAI
THE GIANT-KILLER

I Chronicles 20:4-And it came to pass after this, that there arose was at Gezar (Gob) with the Philistines; at which time **SIBBECHAI** the Hushathite slew Sippai (Saph) that was of the children of the **GIANT**: and they were subdued.

COMPARING DAVID'S LISTINGS OF his 'mighty men' in II Samuel 23 and I Chronicles 11, we find a warrior by the name of Mebunnai, or Sibbechai. I have come to believe these two names are for the same soldier because they fall in the same slot or the same order David gave them in II Samuel 23, and the same order recorded in I Chronicles 11. They both are called Hushathites, the patronymic of the family of Hushah of the tribe of Judah (I Chronicles 4:4), and this is all we know for sure about this mighty man of David:

1. Sibbechai: "the eighth captain for the eighth month was Sibbecai (Sibbechai) the Hushathites of the Zarhites (from Zarah or Zerah, the son of Judah-Numbers 26:20) and in his course were twenty and four thousand." (I Chronicles 27:11) This would have made Sibbechai one of David top dozen generals, responsible for a month of the year in the protection of the borders of Israel!

2. Sibbechai is also recorded as the man who killed a 'giant': "And it came to pass after this, that there was again a battle with the Philistines at

Gob: then Sibbechai (Sibbecai) the Hushathite slew Saph (possibly a brother to Goliath), which was one of the sons of the giant." (II Samuel 21:18 and I Chronicles 20:4) Sibbechai's only call to Biblical fame was at the first Battle at Gob when he took on the giant Saph and killed him, but that event was enough to immortalize Sibbechai in the Word of God. We know very little of this battle; we don't even know how Sibbechai slew Saph, but perhaps that is the way the Lord wanted us to remember Sibbechai. I believe Sibbechai was just one of David's ordinary soldiers at the Battle of Gob, but before the battle was over Sibbechai would go down in Jewish history as a 'giant-killer'! Will we stand in this evil day against the giants that still stalk the land? These giants might not be gigantic in size but in intellect, in position, in power, whose *every imagination of the thoughts of the heart was (is) only evil continually.*" (Genesis 6:5) In the days of Noah they were called 'men of renown', and Jesus warned us that as the days of Noah so would the coming of the Son of God be (Matthew 24:37); for me this includes 'giants'. We too must develop our fighting skills, so like Sibbechai we might take on the 'giants'!

3. Sibbechai means 'Jehovah is intervening', but Mebunnai means 'built up', and it is around that name and meaning I would like to challenge you from this verse in Colossians 2:7: "Rooted and BUILT UP in Him, and stablished in the faith, as ye have been taught, abounding with thanksgiving." As Mebunnai helped David built up the nation of Israel after the civil war with the family of Saul and the countless wars with the enemies that surrounded Israel, so too must we learn to 'built up'!

Dave Egner, writing in an Our Daily Bread article once recorded this: "Scripture portrays the Christian life as a process of growth in which we advance from one stage to the next: from spiritual infancy to maturity, from milk to strong meat, from being rooted in Christ to being firmly established. We may want to be grown up all at once, but we must learn to take one step at a time. I realized this anew as my 16-month-old granddaughter and I were walking along the channel in Muskegon, Michigan. I was in somewhat of a hurry, but Kelsey was not. From her toddler perspective, she had seen a 6-inch-ledge that ran the length of the walkway. Slowly and carefully she climbed on top of the ledge. After standing there triumphantly for a moment, she cautiously stepped back down. It was quite an accomplishment for the little tyke. Then she wanted to make sure she mastered it well. So she a few feet farther down the walk climbed onto the ledge again. I patiently waited for her because I knew this was an important phase of her learning. And I thought, I can learn from her. I need to be sure I've mastered one spiritual discipline before proceeding to one that is more advanced. Then I won't become discouraged in my climb to maturity. Spiritual growth occur a step at a time." One of the dangers often repeated in the Bible (I Corinthians 3:1–3-Hebrews 5:11–14) is the scourge of spiritual stagnation; when the believer doesn't grow but stays the same. We might start out with milk (I Peter 2:2), but we need to grow into strong meat (Hebrews 5:14)! This happens when we are 'built up' in Christ feeding daily on His Word (II Peter 3:18).

Christ said, "I will build my Church." (Matthew 16:18) As Dave Egner watched his granddaughter expand her abilities and boundaries, so too does Christ watch us as we walk through this life. Mr. Egner saw a tiny glimpse of the advancement of his granddaughter during their walk together along that channel in Michigan, so too does Christ see us being built up in Him, even though, like the little girl, we never notice it ourselves. Ours is an observation that is made over time as we realize that we are not the same, our interests are not the same over time. Christ has the ability to see our slightest advancements, or steps enlarging, or interests expanding: growing up is built up! Peter makes an interesting analogy to this concept in his first epistle to the scattered saints (I Peter 1:1). After speaking of the newborn (I Peter 2:2), he speaks of the saints as 'lively stones' being built up as a spiritual house (I Peter 2:5). Ethel Barrett, in her book (It Only Hurts When I Laugh) tells the story of the king of Sparta and his boast to a Greek ambassador of the invincible walls of Sparta. The visitor quickly asked if he might see these walls. The king's reply was that in the morning the Greek ambassador would be taken on a tour of the walls of Sparta. The next morning, to the ambassador's surprise, the king of Sparta took his guest through the gates of the city onto the plains outside the town. Their standing in perfect order and attention was the well-disciplined and world-famous army of Sparta. The king of Sparta pointed to his troops and proclaimed: "There they are! There are the walls of Sparta!" I have come to believe that we too are to be such walls. In the New Testament the Church of Christ is likened to a bride (Ephesians 5), a brotherhood (I Peter 2:17), a body (I Corinthians 12), but also a building (Ephesians 2:21–22). As we speak the Good Lord through His Spirit is building up His 'temple', a temple not made with brick and granite, timber or tile, but 'lively stones', you and me, so as we are built up we are being built in to the building of God!

Believer by believer, Christ too is building up His Church. Has he put you into His building yet? Have you been built up into God's walls yet? If you haven't, my encouragement to you would be to yield to the Master bricklayer, and let him use you to finish His wall (work)! Mebunnai is a good example to us through the meaning of his name, but his other name is just as important (Jehovah is intervening). Only when the Father choses the stone, and only when the Spirit convicts (prepares) the stone, while Jesus be able to take that stone and make it apart of His grand building: the Church! One of the greatest deeds in Christendom is to help build the Church and even when we go up against **'the gates of hell'**; guarded by giants, like Saph, we will always prevail!

45

LAHMI
THE FORMIDABLE GIANT

I Chronicles 20:5-And there was war again with the Philistines; and Elhanan the son of Jair slew **LAHMI** the brother of Goliath the Gittite, whose spear staff was like a weaver's beam.

"THEN HE (DAVID) TOOK his staff in his hand, chose five smooth stones from the stream, put them in the pouch of his shepherd's bag, and with his sling in his hand, approached the Philistine." (I Samuel 17:40 NIV). Have you ever considered why David took five stones out of the Brook of Elah? An interesting answer to that thought provoking question, if not a scriptural one, is because Goliath had four brothers! Whether any of them were at the Battle of Elah, we don't really know, for it isn't until we get to the Third Battle of Gob, much, much later in David's reign, that we even discover that Goliath had brothers. There is speculation that David took the extra stones just in case he missed, but knowing what we know of David, he rarely missed, especially when God was directing the shot. Personally, I have come to the conclusion that this concept is one of the reasons we need to study 'the giants of the Bible'; when Satan makes something, he never makes just one. Goliath had brothers and these brothers like Goliath needed to die!

So did Goliath have four huge brothers just like himself? This might be one of those questions where the admonition of Paul can be applied:

"Let every man be fully persuaded in his own mind." (Romans 14:5) I have become fully persuaded that Goliath (I Samuel 17:4), Ishbibenob (II Samuel 21:16), Saph (II Samuel 21:18), Lahmi (I Chronicles 20:5), and a six-finger monstrosity from Gath (II Samuel 21:20) were all the sons of a giant named Rapha. It is easy to connect the last four because we read: "These four were born to the giant of Gath, and fell by the hand of David, and by the hand of his servants." (II Samuel 21:22) We add to that verse these verses: "…….And Ishibibenob, one of the descendants of Rapha……., "(II Samuel 21:16) and "….Lahmi, the brother of Goliath the Gittite…." (I Chronicles 20:5) and I come to the conclusion that all five giants were related. You also need to consider that David never killed any of the last four giants and yet it speaks of the giant David killed and that could only be Goliath, and for me the connection is made! Also the last giant was actually killed in Gath, Goliath's hometown, and it seems quite clear that we have been dealing with a family of giants!

The Gittites were the people from the Philistine city of Gath, one of the five city-states of Philistia. These five cities had formed a strong confederacy along Israel's western border next to the Mediterranean Sea. Rapha, the Hebrew word for giant, was probably a descendant of the original Rapha who bore the Rephaims (Genesis 14:5). This race of giants had inhabited the Promised Land in a variety of places. Remember, first in the country of Bashan were Moses and Joshua destroyed a giant by the name of OG: "For only Og king of Bashan remained of the remnant of giants." (Deuteronomy 3:11) OG was the only giant left on the east bank of the Jordan, but there were others on the west bank. Remember, second in the city of Hebron were Caleb came up against the descendants of a giant by the name of Anak (Joshua 14:12–15). The Anakims were destroyed by Caleb and his family with the last giants to fall being the descendants of the giant called Arba (Joshua 14:15). Now we have come to the last stronghold of the giants and that being the Philistine town of Gath, for we read: "There was none of the Anakims left in the land of the children of Israel: only in Gaza, in Gath, and in Ashdod, there remained." (Joshua 11:22). Towards the end of Joshua's life he advised the complaining children of Joseph: "If thou be a great people then get thee up to the wood country, and cut down for thyself there in the land of the Perizzites, AND OF THE GIANTS, if Mount Ephraim be too narrow for thee." (Joshua 17:15). So even in the days of Joshua it was a well-known fact that many giants still lived in Canaan because Joshua was probably speaking of the land of the Philistines when he referred to 'the land of the giants', but the Ephraimites wouldn't take on the Philistines, so until David's time there was a mutual respect and despite a few skirmishes during the days of the Judges (Judges 3:31), there was no direct giant conflicts until David meet Goliath on the battlefield of Elah. By that time there seems to be only one family of giants that had survived to the Davidic time and they were located in the town of Gath. (Deuteronomy 2:11)

I have come to believe in the Third Battle of Gob we meet Goliath's 'little brother' or should we simply say 'younger brother'? For not only did Lahmi present a formable size; he also had a formable spear; the most unique aspect given by the writer. If not his brother's spear (we know that David took Goliath's sword (I Samuel 17:51 and 21:9), but there is no mention to Goliath's spear!), one like his brother's spear: "The staff of whose spear was like a weaver's beam." (Compare II Samuel 21:19 and I Samuel 17:7) The author Dake says: "This refers to the wooden handle or part of the spear to which the spearhead was attached. What size it was is not known but it was like the weaver's beam; that is, the part on which the warp is rolled on, or which the cloth was rolling in weaving. Though not mentioned in connection with Lahmi's spear, it does say that Goliath's 'spearhead weighted 600 shekels of iron' (I Samuel 17:70 that is about 24 pounds. It would take quite a man just to carry a weapon with such a heavy head, let alone throw it, or use it affectively in battle." But let us never forget Isaiah 54:17!

David killed Lahmi's brother with Goliath's own sword (I Samuel 17:51), could Elhanan have done the same thing with Lahmi's spear? The Scriptures are silent on just how Elhanan slew Lahmi, but we do have a story from one of David's other mighty men that might just explain my theory: "And (Benaiah) struck down a huge Egyptian. Although the Egyptian had a spear in his hand, Benaiah went against him with a club. He snatched the spear from the Egyptian's hand and killed him with his own spear." (II Samuel 23:21 NIV) Whatever happened at the Third Battle of Gob this we do know that like his brother Goliath, Lahmi was killed in open battle, not by an army, a battalion, or a squad of soldiers, but by an ordinary soldier. Do I believe in divine intervention; certainly I do just like with David, for even though God isn't mentioned His Hand was in it just like David said (I Samuel 17:47). We should never forget that God's ordinary men (I Corinthians 1:26–29) are much better in a fight than any of Satan's super soldiers! Josephus, the famous Jewish historian recorded this fight between Elhanan and Lahmi this way: "After which defeat, the Philistines made war again; and when David sent an army against them, Nephan (Elhanan) his kinsman fought in a single combat with the stoutest of all the Philistines, and slew him, and put the rest to flight." Divine repetition!

David's soldiers were no larger or stronger or more skilled than any other of his soldiers, yet on certain days they performed in extraordinary and spectacular manners, how? I believe in the divine assistance of God because these "giant" battles were really contests between Jehovah and Satan, so when God's name is on the line, God helps! Let us never forget that sin also has many brothers; like covetousness revealing its self in stealing or adultery. We need to be watchful for giant brothers for they are as formable as the original. We also face many formidable foes, but like Elhanan we can also win!

46

ELHANAN
THE GIANT KILLER

II Samuel 21:19-And there was again a battle in Gob with the Philistines, were **ELHANAN** the son of Jaareoregim, a Bethlehemite, slew the brother of Goliath the Gittite, the staff of whose spear was like a weaver's beam.

JUST BECAUSE DAVID KILLED the giant Goliath, it didn't mean that giants were finished. They kept coming because there was a giant for Abishai (II Samuel 21:17), and a giant for Sibbechai (II Samuel 21:18), and a giant for Elhanan, and there will be a giant for us as well, for sin has many brothers and they are all giants. I believe sin is a giant and is best defined by this precept from the pen of Paul in Hebrews 12:1: "Wherefore seeing we are compassed about with so great a cloud of witnesses, let us lay aside every weight, AND THE SIN WHICH DOTH SO EASILY BESET US, and let us run with patience the race that is set before us." How many saints have been deceived into thinking just because Goliath is dead that there are no more giants to fear or face? How many Christians after conquering one bad habit have been trapped by a second brother, equal to or more powerful than the first? We need to remember the precept of Luke 4:13!

Jesus shares this insight into the concept I am trying to illustrate in the life of Elhanan: "When the unclean spirit is gone out of a man, he walketh through dry places, seeking rest, and findeth none. Then he saith, I will return into my house from whence I came out; and when he is come, he findeth it empty, swept, and garnished. Then goeth he, and taketh with himself seven other spirits more wicked than himself, and they enter in and dwell there: and the last state of that man is worse than the first. Even so shall it be also unto this wicked generation." (Matthew 12:43–45) Iniquity has many brothers and each is as formable as the first. At the Battle of Elah, David cut off the head of Goliath, yet many years later David almost got his head cut off by Goliath's brother (II Samuel 21:15–17). It seems each time David and his army attacked Philistia, or was attacked by Philistia there was a giant to face. So it is with us in our battles with sin. I wondered if David thought with each encounter if he was seeing a clone of Goliath, for if they were brothers then they might have looked alike! Dressed in similar armour and carrying familiar weaponry, David and his men might have thought: "Didn't we kill that giant in the last battle?" Yet battle after battle, a recognizable mountain of a man seemed to be at the forefront of battle. On the eve of each of the Battles for Gob stood another giant, another Goliath with a gigantic weapon in hand; another foe, another formable fen just as furious as the one before. There seems to be always one more giant to kill. I found this poem that might help us understand this parallel between giants and sins: *"It's a fight and a hard fight, and a fight to the end. For life is no sleep in the clover; it's a fight for the boy and a fight for the man, and a fight until days are all over."* Remember, our last enemy is death (a giant in and of itself): **"The last enemy that shall be destroyed is death."** (I Corinthians 15:26) So don't think you will get through life without facing this one!

The Indians have a saying: "that when a warrior kills a foe the spirit of that the vanquished enters the victor's heart and adds to his strength for every future struggle." In this thought lies a truth I believe. **As each defeat leaves us weaker, so every victory leaves us stronger!** This seems to be the way it was with David and his mighty men. As each giant fell before them, there seems to always be someone willing to take on the next giant, and in the third battle for Gob that warriors name was Elhanan, which means "God is Gracious". Every time we face a giant on a battlefield and come out of the fight victorious; then God has been gracious! Someone has defined grace as "that action of God by which He withholds deserving penalty and alleviates suffering and distress." The Psalmist wrote of God: "The Lord is merciful and **_gracious_**, slow to anger, and plenteous in mercy." (Psalm 103:8) Moses wrote of God, "And the Lord passed by before him, and proclaimed, The Lord, the Lord God, merciful, and **_gracious,_** longsuffering, and abundant in goodness and truth." (Exodus 34:6) What a gracious God we serve!

As it was in Elhanan's days, so it is today; the graciousness of God should be a source of wonder and awe to every human being on this planet. Despite our rebelliousness and ungratefulness, God has not abandoned His principles of graciousness. Surely, the fight against the giants is a fitting testimony to God's graciousness? What love and what patience He shows towards us in the conditions of today. We speak of the past, but the same gracious Lord is forbearing and forgiving still to all who fight for Him. **We should never forget that God's anger and wrath comes by measure, but God's graciousness and mercy without measure.**

Peter says: "If so be ye have tasted that the Lord is gracious." (I Peter 2:3) I like what Charles Haddon Spurgeon writes in his great Devotional book "Morning and Evening" on the word "if" in this classic verse on grace: "If: then, this is not a matter to be taken for granted concerning every one of the human race. 'If': then there is a possibility and a probability that some may not have tasted that the Lord is gracious. 'If': then this is not a general but a special mercy; and it is needful to enquire whether we know the grace of God by inward experience. There is not spiritual favour which may not be a matter for heart-searching. But while this should be a matter of earnest and prayerful inquiry, no one ought to be content whilst there is any such thing as an 'if' about his having tasted that the Lord is gracious. Advance beyond these dreary 'ifs' abide no more in the wilderness of doubts and fears; cross the Jordan of distrust, and enter the Canaan of peace." Elhanan had no 'ifs' in God when he faced Lahmi!

Today, as we put on our 'dress for success' (Ephesians 6:10–18) against the giants that stalk us, let us be conscience of the fact that despite our past victories over sin yesterday, we will no doubt have to reface its brother today. And because "God is gracious", we will leave the battlefield a victor with another giant lying at our feet defeated. And even after our latest victory, we cannot rest in the afterglow of success, for tomorrow another giant will block our path to a righteous life. If we read carefully the stories of II Samuel 21 we count three giants in three battles (II Samuel 21:15–19), and yet when David's army attacked the stronghold of the giants (Gath) there is still another brother of his archenemy waiting to take him on (II Samuel 21:20–21). If this is true of David, let us not be surprised if this is no true of us. Sin like giants has many brothers, and thought they might have different names: Covetousness, Wickedness, Murderous, Fornication,

Blasphemy, Disobedience, Maliciousness, Unrighteousness, and so many more; each must be faced and destroyed before they are no longer a threat to us. For me the story of Elhanan is the story of a victor not a victim. So too with us as we rely on the graciousness of God we too can be a winner in the confrontations with sin and its evil brothers, but it is **'the sin that so easily bests us'** that is our giant. It knows our weaknesses and it waits it chance, but let us never forget that Elhanan (God is Gracious) is on our side. It is when we take up His graciousness that we can be confident that our 'giant' sin will be defeated! Let us never forget this from the pen of the psalmist: "Mine enemies would daily swallow me up, for they be many that fight against me, O thou most High." (Psalm 56:2) But every one of them will fall when faced with grace!

47

THE LAST GIANT OF GATH
THE FINGER GIANT

II Samuel 21:20-And there was yet a battle in Gath, where was a man of great stature, that had on every hand six fingers, and on every foot six toes, four and twenty in number; and he was also born to the **GIANT**.

PAUL TELLS US THAT in the spiritual struggle our foes are many: "For we wrestle not against flesh and blood, but against *principalities*, against *powers*, against *rulers* of the darkness of this world, and **against spiritual wickedness in high places**." (Ephesians 6:12) Principalities, powers, politicians, and the prince of the power of the air (Ephesians 2:2) are the most recognized enemies of the Christian soldier in the Bible, but there are more: there are 'giants'! Most of us will not have to face a physically huge foe, or a deformed foe, but some will, and it is for them that I write this article about the last giant of Gath, the final giant to be defeated by David and his mighty men!

There are places were the Christian should fear to go, not because you don't have faith in God, but because of what is there. Places were the wicked one has controlled, dominated, and demon infested for a very long time: a place like Gath; such places, when you go you are in peril for your life; a place like the jungles of Ecuador. I doubt Nate Saint, Roger Youderian, Ed McCully, Peter Fleming, or Jim Elliot thought they were going to die taking the Gospel to the Auca people, but like Jonathan (II Samuel 21:21) they were going into Gath and the last giant of Gath will fight to the end. Though few and isolated now, it has been the courage and bravery of men like Jonathan that these strongholds of Satan have been conquered: strongholds like Gath of Philistia. And though the Auca Five didn't seen the conquest they set the stage for their wives and sisters to see the Auca people come to a saving knowledge of Christ. For David and his mighty men, Gath was the last home of a diabolical gigantic race, a superhuman race of devilish people that needed to be conquered, and in order to conquer such a place you have to go!

As we have highlighted and underlines again and again the soldier of Christ must endure hardness (II Timothy 2:3): hard times, hard places, and hard enemies. When you fight a giant on his home turf it will be a hard and difficult struggle. I found this story in one of my favorite devotional book by Mrs. Charles Cowper, "Streams in the Desert":

"'Die hard, my men, die hard!' shouted Colonel Inglis of the 57th Division to his men on the heights behind the River Albuhera. The regiment would be nicknamed 'the die-hards' after this encounter with the enemy. The tale may have been forgotten, but the name lives on; and in spite of foolish uses, it is a great name. It challenges us. We are called to be the Lord's 'die-hards', to whom can be committed any kind of trial of endurance, and who can be counted upon to stand firm no matter what happens. It is written of Oliver Cromwell: 'He strove to give his command so strict a unity that in no crisis would it crack.' With this aim in view, he made his 'ironsides'! The result of that discipline was seen not only in victory but in defeat; for his troops, 'though they were beaten and routed, presently railed again and stood in good order until they received new orders.' This is the spirit that animates all valiant life; to be strong in will, to strive, to seek, to find, and not to yield is all that matters. Failure or success, as the world understands these words, is of no eternal account. To be able to stand steady in defeat is in itself a victory. There is no tinsel about that kind of triumph. No man is sure of the outcome of a battle (like the Auca Five) fought against a giant in his hometown, but in Christ we are always 'more than conquerors through Him' (Romans 8:37) even in the giant's last stronghold!"

What makes this last battle with the giants so interesting to me is the fact the giant is the oddest one of them all; unnamed by the author, but he felt that he had to describe the uniqueness of this man of great stature. Josephus, the famous Hebrew historian, writing on the giants of Hebron describes them this way: "There were then still left the race of giants, who had bodies so large, and countenances so entirely different from other men, that they were surprising to the sight, and terrible to the hearing." This might help us understand the strangeness of the last giant of Gath. It might help us to explain why the men of Saul's army at the Battle of Elah were so frightened at the blasphemy of Goliath (I Samuel 17:11)? There sight and sound was so unnatural, they were almost not human? Josephus makes one last interesting observation on 'giants' in his writings: "The bones of these men are still shown to this day, unlike to any credible relations to other men!" Josephus was claiming that the bones of the giants of Hebron were still being examined nearly 1400 years after (which was during the age of Christ) Caleb killed them. Was one of the unique features having an extra finger on each hand, and an extra toe on each foot? These giants were so unique that people had kept their bones because of their oddity. Talk about not wanting to meet someone in a back alley on a dark night!

In all my study, I have not found one giant to ever be an ally of God, or God's people; they were all foes, enemies of God and God's chosen race. I also never found a giant in any of God's armies throughout history. Even Samson, the world's strongest man, was not a giant, a man of superior height and size, for we learn through a study of Samson's life (Judges 13–16) that Samson go his supernatural strength through the Spirit of God, not his makeup or muscles. The giant of Gath was 'a man of great stature'! This is the difference between Satan's Super Soldiers and God's warriors. Satan produces fear by size (Numbers 13:33), but God produces faith by His Spirit: **"Not by might, nor by power, but by my Spirit saith the Lord."** (Zechariah 4:6) We should conclude right now that our foes will always seem bigger, better, and more boastful (prideful): "...and he defied Israel." (II Samuel 21:21) Just like Goliath defied Israel (I Samuel 17:45) I believe Jonathan, like David, was provoked by this boasting giant. Remember David words at the Battle of Elah: "For who is this uncircumcised Philistine that he should defy the armies of the Living God?" (I Samuel 17:26) and like David, Jonathan was just a young man at the Battle of Gath (the son of David brother Shimeah-I Samuel 16:6–10). So despite his unusual shape (more fingers and toes than the normal person-II Samuel 21:20), Jonathan, like David, was willing to attack and kill this monstrosity from Gath. (We will deal more with Jonathan the giant killer in our next chapter.)

Unparalleled insolence has always been a characteristic of God's foes, our foes! Being the last giant, this freak of Satan had either seen or heard of the death of all the other giants (a careful read of II Samuel 21:15–22 will convince you that the other giants named in that passage, and Goliath himself were all brothers!), yet instead of being humbled, this giants was more defiant (II Samuel 21:22)! If Satan was their creator then it is not surprising that they like their father would be so prideful because this was the trait of Lucifer (Isaiah 14:12–15) in heaven. So it is with all our foes, but we can boldly proclaim that we have yet to find a giant that ever won once over a man of God in the Bible. They can taunt, they can tease, and they can tempt us into fearing them or doubting God, but in reality all they are doing is bagging and boasting to their own destruction. As with the other giant-killers before him this giant was not match for God's giant-killer; _**the Lord had given**_ Israel Jonathan for this! And as with the Auca, they too were conquered!

48

JONATHAN
THE GIANT-KILLER

II Samuel 21:21-And when he defied Israel, **JONATHAN** the son of Shimeah the brother of David slew him.

JONATHAN WAS DAVID NEPHEW. Now we know another one of David's brother's names as only three are given in I Samuel 16:6–9 account of Jesse's sons being brought before the prophet Samuel. In the Biblical account it seems only fitting that the first giant of Gath would fall to a son of Jesse and the last giant of Gath would fall by one of Jesse's grandsons. Jonathan simply means 'Jehovah is given'. I have come to the belief as you surely have noticed by now that *'**the Lord wrought a great victory**'* and *'**the battle is the Lord's**'* in respect of the struggles with the 'giants'. For ever giant Satan produced, Jehovah raised up a giant-killer to take care of the matter. It reminds me of the times of the judges when Israel needed someone to deliver them, it says: "Nevertheless the Lord rasied up judges, which delivered them out of the hand of those that spoiled them." (Judges 2:16) Jehovah did the same during the time of the giants, and when it came to killing the last giant of Gath the giant-killer called on was a young man named Jonathan.

What should the giant of Gath tell us about facing fearful foes on their own doorstep? What should the death of the last giant tell us about the end of the greatest giant of them all, death? And what should the Battle of Gath tell us of the conflicts yet to come with giants? First, we must conclude that it is folly to fear that which only glories in flesh and blood. If we are foolish enough to wrestle in flesh and blood we will be defeated by Satan's giants every time (Ephesians 6:12), but our fight is not in flesh and blood but in the Spirit, and we are promised: **"Greater is He that is in me than he that is in the world."** (I John 4:4) Read carefully theses instruction by Paul-II Corinthians 10:3–4! Second, we must conclude that like the last giant, our last enemy, one of the greatest giants we face, death, will also be destroyed (I Corinthians 15:26). There is an appointed time for all giants to die, including Satan (Revelation 20:10). I like the way Ezekiel describes their destruction: "And they shall not lie with the mighty that are fallen of the uncircumcised, which are gone down to hell with their weapons of war; and they have laid their swords under their heads, but their iniquities shall be upon their bones, though they were the terror of the mighty in the land of the living." (Ezekiel 32:27) What a great description of the end of a gigantic warrior. There was and still is only a season for giants, and when Christ finally destroys them, we will see them no more, for theirs is a different destination than ours. (Matthew 25:41) Lastly, we must conclude that the most powerful enemies will probably be faced in life's final battles. I write this while my father of 91 is facing his toughest foes in a VA home in northern Maine. A man of great health and strength well into his mid-80's Dad is now being subjected to weakness that requires help, and a mental disability that is taking away his memory and his recognition of family. He is confused and paranoid, enemies he never through he would face, foes his family never thought he would face. A simple study of the lives of the saints in the Scriptures will reveal that life's battles get tougher and life's foes get more numerous. Satan will always keep a giant in reserve to face us in life's final skirmish!

The greatest teaching that might come out of the life of this giant-killer is found in the meaning of his name. The death of every giant is a gift of God, a gift to the people of God; one less giant to face. The irony of this reality is illustrated by this story out of the life of the great English preacher, Charles Haddon Spurgeon. In his classic book, "All of Grace", he writes of:

> "….a minister who went to the home of a poor woman to give her some money that she desperately needed; when he knocked at her door, she did not answer. He felt sure she was home, so he knocked again. Still no response! After more knocking, he left. On Sunday, he saw her in church and said, 'I called at your home last Friday. I supposed you were not at home, for I knocked several times and you did not answer. I had some money for you.' 'What time were

you there?' she asked. 'About noon,' the minister replied. 'Oh, dear,'
said the woman, 'I heard you. But I did not answer. I thought it was
my landlord calling for the rent.'"

How many of us resist opening the door to Gath because we fear the giant
behind the door? Only to realize later that God had come to show us that
the last of the giants of Gath will die at our hand!

Following a recent reading of a book about the great Protestant reformer Martin Luther, the author of the book related how despite Luther's
fame and faithfulness, he still had great personal internal struggles to the
very end of his life. The words that strengthened Luther most in the last
battles were words from his own pen:
"A safe stronghold our God shall be, a trusty shield and weapon. He'll help
us clear from all the ill that hath us now overtaken. And were this world
all devil's over, and watching to devour us. We lay it not to heart so sore,
not they can overpower us. And though they take our life, God's honor,
children, wife, yet is their profit small, these things shall vanish all."
F. B. Meyer wrote this in his book "Great Verses Through the Bible":

> "God's best things are gifts. Light, air, natural beauty, elasticity of
> the spirits, the sense of vigorous health, human live, and, above
> all, his only begotten Son. Among all other gifts is there one to
> be compared to this? The living spring of eternal life, which Jesus
> opened up in our hearts, and which so greatly differs from the pit
> of outward ordnance, is an altogether unspeakable bestowment.
> Nothing can purchase it. If a man would give all the substance of
> his house for it, it would be utterly condemned. It must be received
> as a gift, or not at all. God's gifts must be asked for. 'Thou wouldest
> have asked, and he would have given.' This is the law of heaven.
> Prayer is a necessary link between the divine hand that gives and
> the human heart that receives. We have not, because we ask not.
> There is nothing in our Lord's words of the dreamy and languid
> pietism which refuses to ask because it will not dictate to the per-
> fect wisdom of God."

Have you asked for Gath yet and the giant that lives behind its walls?

I know not if Jonathan asked to be the last giant killer or not (he no
doubt had heard of the exploits of his uncle at the Battle of Elah all his
life), but I know that God just loves to answer our prayers when it comes
to gigantic problem, titanic trials, and giant needs. Because when we defeat our last foe God will be honored. Let us remember today that God is
our strength and our shield and our stronghold when we are fighting our

enemy in his last bastion. Fear not, nor faint, nor fret, for we are promised victory through our Lord and Saviour Jesus Christ (I Corinthians 15:57). Even if that final foe is a giant with ties to the wicked one himself: "Until I make thy foes thy footstool." (Acts 2:35) Giant footstools are made in Gath. We are not told how Jonathan slew this giant, but like the other giant-killers before him this giant was not match for God's giant-killer; *the Lord had given* Israel Jonathan for this!

49

TO KILL A GIANT

I Chronicles 20:8-These were born unto the **GIANT** of Gath; and they fell by the hand of David, and by the hand of his servants.

As WE NEAR THE end of our study of Satan's Super Soldiers, better known in the Bible as 'giants', it is time for me to share with you a few final observation in this overview of what I have discovered about Scriptural 'giants'. To the best of my ability, I have shown you all the named 'giants' in the Bible as well as a few unnamed 'giants' that can be clearly see in Scripture. We have highlighted the spiritual lessons we have learned on the way and we have underlined each giant encountered and we have re-fought each battle in which a giant participated and was slain. In this devotional I would like to give to you five (we might call them 'the five stones' that slew Satan's super soldiers) final precepts I have learned and we will put them under the caption: 'to kill a giant'!

First precept: "NOT ALL GIANTS ARE SLAIN IN THE SAME BATTLE"! I Corinthians 10:13-"There hath no temptation taken you but such as is common to man: but God is faithful, who will not suffer you to be tempted above that ye are able; but will with the temptation also make a way of escape, that ye may be able to bear it." Despite the fact that 'the giant of Gath' had five sons; they were all killed in separate battles. In all my study, only in the Battle of Hebron could I honestly say that more than one giant was killed (Joshua 14:14 and Judges 1:10). Even then, if you remember, it was my conclusion that the three giants of Anak were located in three cities: Hebron and Debir and Anab. I believe that God will never allow our enemy to become any bigger than we can handle in a single fight. God will never allow our foe to get any bigger than we can defeat in a single struggle. God will always make a way of escape from any adversary that will tempt us into defeat. My conclusion: what we can slay, what we can defeat, and what we can resist is as much as the Lord will allow to face us!

Second precept: "NOT ALL GIANTS USE THE SAME STRATEGY AGAINST US"! II Corinthians 2:11-"Lest Satan should get an advantage of us: for we are not ignorant of his devices." 'Devices' is found here in the plural, and we have learned in our study of the giants that each giant had his own special weapon. Remember the Rephaims used their size; the Anakims used fear; Goliath used taunting; Ishbibenob had a 'new' sword; Lahmi used his brother's reputation, and the three giants of Hebron used their mighty walls. In a recent study of the Gospel of Luke I uncovered at least a dozen diabolical devices the Devil used against the Lord during his lifetime. This is why we need to study carefully the Bible and search for these devices; the Devil's tricks and deceptions to defeat us. We in turn will also learn how to defeat him, just like the giant-killers did, because.......

Third precept: "NOT ALL GIANTS ARE KILLED IN THE SAME WAY"! Ephesians 6:11-"Put on the whole armour of God that ye may be able to stand against the wiles of the Devil." We must not only study the tactics of the 'giants', but we must also study the techniques of the giant-killers. That has been the purpose of this book to uncover both and learn the strategies needed to fight our own giant. We might not know how all the giants died, but there seems to be no duplication of the methods used. We know that the first 'giants' were destroyed by water in the Great Flood and probably some just died of old age, but we know that Goliath was brought down with a single stone and killed by his own sword. The key for me in this is simply adaptability. We are to put on the 'whole' armour of God. Each piece of the armour is used in the spiritual struggle can be used to resist a specific assault of the Devil, and it is within the complete package that we are able to take on all 'the wiles of the Devil'. If you leave on piece behind, it might just be the piece you need that day. We must be fully prepared from all sides and in all situations and by all means and through all methods to resist the attack of Satan's super soldiers. The day you leave the shield of faith at home will be the very day Satan's fires one of his fiery darts at you (Ephesians 6:16)!

Forth precept: "NOT ALL GIANTS ARE SLAIN BY THE SAME PERSON"! I Corinthians 1:27-"….and God hath chosen the weak things of the world to confound the things which are mighty." Let me give to you my list of named 'giants' and named giant-killers:

Satan's Super Soldiers	God's Ordinary Warrior
Og	Moses
Ahiman	Caleb
Sheshai	Joshua
Talmai	Othniel
Goliath	David
Ishibibenob	Abishai
Saph	Sibbechai
Lahmi	Elhanan

And then there was that six-finger and toes giant that was killed by Jonathan! You will notice that the names of Rapha, Arba, and Anak are missing from my list, for I believe they were taken care of by God Himself. Sometimes God takes care of giants before we face them, but at other times He leaves them to us. I love the story of Peter and John at the Beautiful Gate (Acts 3:1–7) when they encountered a man born lame. How many times had Jesus passed this man by because it tells us that he had been laid there daily for years? Yes, Jesus does leave for us certain battles and we must fight them with His help!

Fifth precept: "NOT ALL WARRIORS WILL FACE THE SAME GI-ANT"! Galatians 6:5-"For every man shall bear his own burdens." Despite the title of this book being Satan's Super Soldiers, the theme of this book has been God's Mighty Warriors. In my study of David I have been compiled to look at his 'mighty men'. In my research, I have come to the conclusion that of the 1,300,000 in David's army (II Samuel 24:9) only 105 fall under the caption of 'mighty men' and of those 105 warriors only five were giant-killer (note the four listed above and to that list we can number Benaiah for he slew a giant Egyptian with his own spear-II Samuel 23:20–21). I find no man in the Bible to have slain two giants, even David! The battles I face in life and the giants I face might not be the same for you. Then there are those that have no battles and fight no giants. Our responsibility isn't to determine which battles or which giants we face, but to simply be prepared for both; fight or not (II Timothy 3:17).

I don't know if these simple observations about Satan's super soldiers will help you or not, but for me in the ongoing battle called life; I am encouraged by the truth that has been revealed to me in this particular Biblical study. I feel I at least understand what it will take to overcome gigantic obstacles, gigantean situation and gigantesque foes. I know through the Bible that no matter where a giant might come from that he is defeatable because the fight against giants is God's battle and I am one of His warriors!

50

THE LAST GIANT TO FALL
LUCIFER

Isaiah 14:12, 15-How art thou fallen from heaven, O **Lucifer**, son of the morning! How art thou cut down to the ground, which didst weaken the nations.......
Yet thou shalt be brought down to hell, to the sides of the pit.

HE HAS COME TO be known by many names: "......the great dragon...
that old serpent...called the Devil and Satan..." (Revelation 12:9) but God
called him Lucifer, the Son of the Morning. I am going to call him 'the last
giant' in this chapter!

Lucifer was created the most beautiful, and I believe the most powerful, of the entire heavenly host, called angels. His was a place of honor in the
realm of heaven because I believe he was God's first creation. Lucifer means
'daystar' for his brilliance was even seen in the daytime, like the bright stars
we can even see in the light of day. With Gabriel and Michael, Lucifer was
named one of the archangels and the three made up God's inner circle in
God's glory. I have come to believe like Peter, James, and John on earth;
Lucifer, Gabriel, and Michael were in heaven. Remember, in a crowd of
'giants' only a titan stands out and Lucifer was one of those heavenly titans,
a giant of an angel.

Then came a moment in eternity past when God heard in the mind
of Lucifer: "**I will** ascend into heaven (some think that Lucifer wasn't in
heaven at the time but on a new planet (earth) created by God), **I will** exalt

my throne (some think that Lucifer already had a throne on earth) above the stars (angels-Daniel 12:3) of God: **I will** set also upon the mount of the congregation, in the sides of the north: **I will** ascend above the heights of the clouds; **I will** be like the most High." (Isaiah 14:13–14) From that very moment God's chief angel became heaven's greatest adversary (what Satan means)! But Lucifer didn't fall alone, for from his evil thoughts and diabolical persuasion he drew many of the celestial angels to his side: "And his tail drew the third part of the stars of heaven, and did cast them to the earth." (Revelation 12:4). A third of the heavenly host was cast out of heaven with Lucifer, and Christ saw them fall: "I beheld Satan as lighting fall from heaven." (Luke 10:18) Note, he was not Lucifer (daystar) any longer, but Satan (adversary). With a mighty army of demonic angels, Lucifer turned into the Devil, and the angels became demons, and the course of history was cast for the rest of time.

No longer fit to remain in the presence of God, the Lord unleashed His angelic army against Lucifer's horde: "And there was war in heaven: Michael and his angels fought against the dragon, and the dragon fought and his angels, and prevailed not, neither was their place found any more in heaven." (Revelation 12:7–8) There are some that believe that this war hasn't happened yet but will take place during the Great Tribulation time, but whether then or in the past this is a great description of what happened to Lucifer when he first fell. So where to send the wicked cherubim? From the prince among angels to "...the prince of the power of the air...." (Ephesians 2:2), and the spirit that now works in the children of the disobedience. From God's adviser, Lucifer became our accuser: "....for the accuser of our brethren is cast down, which accused them before our God day and night." (Revelation 12:10) It was in this capacity that Satan hounded and harassed and hunted Job. (Job 1–2) Note again that it is Satan that presents himself to God not Lucifer. This same Satan is hunting us to this very day (I Peter 5:8)!

Because of God's ultimate plan of redemption for the human race through the sacrifice of His only begotten Son on Calvary, God even used Satan to tempt man, cause his fall, and then in a dramatic move that backfired on Lucifer, used the Devil himself to bring about the death of Christ; (Luke 22:3) which ultimately became the head wound prophesied by God in the Garden of Eden (Genesis 3:15). Despite his bold proclamation of being in charge, Lucifer has been a simple pawn in a global chess match ever since he was put on the board. It has become my belief that Satan's Super Soldiers were also just pawns of God. I still remember the day I found this acknowledgement by God: "Now these are the nations which the Lord left to prove Israel by them....namely, five lords of the Philistines..." (Judges 3:1–3) Who lived among the five city-states of the Philistines? "There was none of the Anakims left in the land of the children of Israel: only in Gaza, in Gath, and in Ashdod, there remained." (Joshua 11:22) Giants and Lucifer, just pawns!!!

Even at Lucifer's downfall God foretold his end: "Yet thou shalt be brought down to hell....!" This is "the everlasting fire, prepared for the devil and his angels." (Matthew 245:41) Lucifer's present day freedom to roam "...to and fro in the earth, and walking up and down in it" (Job 1:7) is only for a season. When his usefulness is over, he will be cast "...into the Lake of Fire....and shall be tormented day and night forever and ever." (Revelation 20:10) Lucifer's destiny is just a matter of time, and his destination is prepared and waiting for him. In David's great lamentation following the death of Saul and his best friend Jonathan, David asks this question: "How are the mighty fallen?" (II Samuel 1:19) There will be no greater fall in all of recorded history greater than the fall of Lucifer. From the first of God's creations and a powerful position in the celestial heavens to a permanent place in hell; no creature has fallen farther. There is no height or distance greater than the height and distance between these two spots in God's creation!

Despite his constant defeats through history and his ultimate defeat in history, Lucifer has had his success stories. These 'infamous instruments' (Satan's Super Soldiers) were used to disrupt the lives of the righteous, delay the works of God, disturb the faith of believers, and deceive the world into unrighteous living. The Devil has used many a device down through time to work his wickedness, but his most successful device has been his instruments of unrighteousness. Men and women who have been sold out to the cause of Satan and his few pleasures. It has been the purpose of this book to remind you of Satan's most infamous devices: the Rephaims and the Anakims. They have all met their end, but their duplicates are still live today. We often forget that wickedness reproduces just like righteousness. That is why we should never be ignorant of them!

We have been forewarned by the Scripture (Ephesians 4:27) and forearmed by the Spiritual armor (Ephesians 6:10–18). As the saints of old battled and faced their 'giant', we must battle (James 4:7) and face our 'giant': the last of the giants, Satan himself. As with our brethren of old, we too have been given by God the ability to detect and deflect his attack (Ephesians 6:16). We have traced the Biblical biographies of Satan's Super

Soldiers, but the greatest of them all is Satan. Through this study we have seen his tactics lest he should get an advantage of us (II Corinthians 2:11). Though the last giant fell at Gath by the hand of one of David's men, the original giant, the last giant is still 'stacking through the land'; that is until he too will face his fate at the Battle of Jerusalem (Revelation 20:7–10). The last giant to fall will be taken out when he tries to reclaim the earth after the millennium kingdom (Revelation 20:6), but like with all of his other direct confrontations with the Almighty, he will fall again, but this time he will not recover from this fall like he seemingly did after his fall from grace in eternity past. Until then, we must be sober and vigilant, watchful and cautious (I Peter 5:8) because the last giant is still on the attack.

POSTLUDE

SATAN'S SUPER SOLDIERS
WERE WIMPS

II Samuel 21:22-These four were born of the **GIANT** of Gath, and fell by the hand of David, and by the hand of his servants.

LIKE MOST, I HAVE for a long time been deceived by the Devil and his promoters into thinking that he and his angels are tough; that his super soldiers were super, but after this study I have come to another conclusion. I still, however, agree with Martin Luther, the great reformer, when he wrote in his classic Church hymn, "A Mighty Fortress is our God", these words: **_"For still our ancient foe doth seek to work us woe, his craft and power are great and armed with cruel hate, on earth is not his equal."_** But after this research and journey into one of Satan's greatest creations, I have come to the persuasion that Satan and his soldiers were and are really **'wimps'**!

'Wimp' is a new word for me and a new word for anybody of my age. I never heard the word until my son Scott started using it quite a few years ago. Scott was a sportsman and excelled in just about every sport he tried (during his high school basketball career he scored nearly 1200 points). Today he is an exceptional golfer (I wrote this before my son passed away from liver and lung cancer at the age of 39!) and for all these years when he saw someone acting timidly in a sport when being confronted he called them a **'wimp'**. It was Scott's word for anyone that should have been able to do better, but didn't live up to the expectations expected! James tells us:

"Resist the devil and he will flee from you." (James 4:7) This Scripture really puts the Devil and his demons in their place. Martin Luther, before he finished writing his wonderful song, also put the Devil in his place: **"The prince of darkness grim, we tremble not for him, his rage we can endure, for lo his doom is sure, ONE LITTLE WORD SHALL FELL HIM."** And now we know that Satan's Super Soldiers were also easily brought down. Whether a single stone or a single soldier, each and every giant recorded in the Bible when confronted (resisted) was easily defeated, and this principle and precept can still be applied today because they were all **'wimps'** still, really!

So we need not be deceived any longer by the roar of the devil, the giants of Satan, or the rage of the old serpent, for that is all it is 'hot-air', super-sized, false boasting. In this study we found that Satan and his warriors have had **'wimpish'** tendencies. My first case in point is the 'giants' before the Flood. In the Garden of Eden who did Satan attack first, Adam or Eve? You know the answer, he went after the 'weaker vessel' (I Peter 3:7) first, and then the devil used Eve to attack Adam. For years we have been giving the Devil credit for a bold plan, an ingenious move when in reality it was a sign that he was really a **'wimp'**! A bold, brave devil would have taken on Adam, why didn't he? My conclusion: he wasn't smart, he was scared! The same was true of the 'giants' he created to corrupt mankind; who did they pick on 'women' (Genesis 6:4). We give them too much credit for corrupting the pre-flood world. When only facing the weakest of mankind, they were called 'mighty men', but when they took on God they were destroyed with H2O!!!!!

My second case in point is the 'giants' after the Flood. Let us start with Satan's first attack on Israel as they neared the gates of Canaan. Maybe, you are not as familiar with this one as some of the others: "Remember what Amalek did unto thee by the way when ye were come forth out of Egypt. How he met thee by the way and smote ***the hindmost*** of there even all that were feeble behind thee, when thou wast faint and weary and feared not God." (Deuteronomy 25:17–18) Satan was the father of all the nations of Canaan including the 'giants', and besides picking on women he loves to pick on the weak. Why do you think the devil waited 40 days before tackling Jesus? (Matthew 4:1–3) He didn't even have a chance when Christ was weak and hungry, but that has been Satan's strategy from the very beginning and it continues today because the Devil is a **'wimp'**. Like with Jesus, we have the Holy Spirit (remember Jesus got the Spirit just before the wilderness temptations -Matthew 3:16–17), and with the Holy Spirit in us: "Ye are of God, little children, and have overcome them: because greater is He that is in you, than he that is in the world." (I John 4:4) Remember the story of David when the giant attacked when David was weak (II Samuel 21:15–17). The giants learned that David was formable when he was a lad (I Samuel 17), so they waited until he was weak. Have you ever noticed the same is true when you come under your worst satanic attacks? **Wimps**, plain **wimps** without the strength or power to attack David, Jesus, or us when we are strong (Ephesians 6:10–11)! We call them smart, wise when in reality they are weak and they know it. Satan knows that he must honor James 4:7, so he attacks when we are too weak to resist. That is why the Bible gives illustration after illustration of the prey of Satan and his followers: the weakest among us. Only a wimp waits to pick off a weak opponent. The Amalekites found the Danites (Numbers 2:3) to strong, so they attacked the widows, the children, the sick, the stragglers in the Israelite column; those in the rear! Satan has been doing this since the beginning and continues to do it today because he is a **'wimp'**!

The great news is that even the weak can resist. The smallest and weakest among us can still quote Scripture like Jesus did (Matthew 4:4, 7, 10). But the weak need help and that is way Paul wrote to the Church at Thessalonica: "Support the weak!" (I Thessalonians 5:14) The weak have always been the primary target of evil, but God's formula is a simple one: 1) *resist*, 2) *recite the Word*, and 3) *remember just say no*! Satan likes to be called by many names (Lucifer, Satan, Apollyon), but the one name he has kept hid is **'Wimp'**! So just say no, he can't resist it (one little word will fall him-as Luther wrote). Just recite a Bible verse, he can't resist it. He has no answer for God's words whether by the lips of Christ or through the lips of a Christian. He's a **'wimp'** and he can't overcome what God has always limited him too. Remember, Satan had to get permission from God to attack a single man, Job (Job 1–2), why? He is a **wimp**, he fears God and he fears touching anything or anyone that God claims as his own, and as for his infamous instruments the giants, they too proved themselves to be **'wimps'** in every way!

Despite their reputation, their renown, the 'giants' were but puppets in the hand of the puppeteer, Satan. The Devil loves to us others to do his dirty work and he continues this practice to this day, but the limitations of Satan are also the limitations of Satan's soldiers. Warning to one of Satan's puppets; when your usefulness is over Satan will discard you like he did the last giants of Gath. Our verse above is the last "giant" verse in the Bible. And as we saw in our last chapter, even the Devil's days are numbered. The infamous giants were a sight to behold, but they were 'paper tigers' at best. Oh, they did have a few hollow victories over the faithless and fearful, but when they were confounded by the bold and brave they were **'wimps'** at best. I still believe we need 'giant-killers' in the Church of God today; men and women who will stand up to the devil and his devilish ways; resisters that will recite the Bible and say no to the **wimp** of all **wimps**! We have been given in this study example after example of how it is done and let us last remember that God never put any armor on our back (Ephesians 6:10–18). We are to face giants and the devil and by simple standing up to them we will set them to flight!

www.ingramcontent.com/pod-product-compliance
Lightning Source LLC
Chambersburg PA
CBHW060337100426
42812CB00003B/1027